I0340945

Little Ninjas Guitar Method Book

Written by Michael Gumley

Copyright © 2023 Michael Gumley

All rights reserved. No part of this book may be reproduced in any form or by any electronic or mechanical means, including information storage and retrieval systems, without permission in writing from the publisher.

Editing by Michael Gumley
Front Cover Image by Michael Gumley
Book Layout & Design by Michael Gumley
All Musical Examples were written and/or arranged by the author with the exception of the riffs and melodies provided here under the fair use act for educational purposes. All rights belong to the copyright owner.

Printed & Bound in Australia by GVP Education Publications
First Edition printed in November 2021
This Edition printed in June 2023
Published by GVP Education Pty Ltd
80 Raleigh St, Essendon, Vic, 3040

Warning!

Unauthorised Photocopying, Recreation, or Distribution is Prohibited

© Guitar Ninjas
Little Ninjas Guitar Method Book
www.GuitarNinjas.com.au

Contents

Introduction...1

Key Concepts For Teachers & Parents............................ 2

Getting Started On Guitar.......................................9

Warmups...25

Melodies...33

Riffs...43

Chords & Progressions... 53

Rhythms..61

Practice Logs...74

© Guitar Ninjas
Little Ninjas Guitar Method Book
www.GuitarNinjas.com.au

Welcome To The Little Ninjas Guitar Book

Little Ninjas is a special version of Guitar Ninjas adapted for children aged 5-8 years old.

People often ask me if their child is too young to start learning guitar. The answer is both yes and no.

Yes, your child is too young to play the guitar to the same standard that you hear professional musicians play on the recordings found on CDs, Youtube videos and the radio.

But no, your child is not too young to learn. We can still achieve great results by redefining what success looks like at their current level of development and adapting our approach to what is achievable at this level.

In short, we don't teach a 5-year-old the same way we would teach a 10-year-old, a teenager, or an adult, and that's why we get such great results.

Unfortunately, many guitar teachers and music schools make the mistake of ignoring the needs of younger learners instead of adapting their teaching methods to suit the individual student. We believe that by tailoring our lessons to what young children can accomplish during these early years, we can achieve much better results and help them have much more fun in the process.

Little Ninjas takes a unique approach. We focus on gradually building important skills and basic concepts while adding complexity over time. Our goal is to foster a love and appreciation for music so that children enjoy their lessons and stay committed to learning the guitar. Our ultimate aim is to lay the foundation for them to become great guitar players in time.

We believe in finding a balance between having fun and achieving results. Our Little Ninjas receive all the necessary support for their age, which helps them establish a strong foundation as they grow physically and cognitively and improve their musical knowledge and technical skills.

Let's embark on an exciting musical journey with Little Ninjas!

The Karate Belt System

At Guitar Ninjas, we use a Karate-inspired system to help young learners advance and improve their guitar playing. Students follow a series of 9 curriculum books and earn a new guitar strap each time they move up to the next level.

This system provides an effective and organized way of learning. We have a simple checklist to track student progress and set milestones for them to achieve. Each time a student levels up, they receive a new belt, a new book, and a certificate to recognize their accomplishments.

Based on our experience with Guitar Ninjas, we noticed that younger students sometimes took longer to progress through the initial stages, which could lead to a loss of motivation. In response to this feedback, we created a special program called Little Ninjas for children aged 5-7 years old.

Little Ninjas is designed to work at a pace that suits young learners. It allows them to advance through the levels more quickly while still experiencing consistent progress and rewards, which are important when teaching young children.

The Little Ninjas program has been simplified to include one book that is broken into three levels. As they make progress, they will receive different coloured bands or badges which can be pinned or tied to their white belts to show their progress.

As students age up they will be advanced to the main program and entered into a more advanced class than total beginners matching their age.

Come join us on the exciting journey of levelling up with the Karate Belt System we use at Little Ninjas!

The Challenges

In our curriculum books, we have included challenges and checklists as an important feature. To move up to the next level, students simply need to complete all the requirements listed for that level. We have designed our method in a way that allows students to focus more on the areas they enjoy, without being held back by skills they find difficult or less motivated to practice.

To make practising more enjoyable, we have created a variety of challenges. These challenges provide students with short and specific objectives that can be achieved within a single practice session. This not only keeps students motivated to practice, but it also makes it easier for parents to encourage their kids by saying "*try to complete one more challenge*" instead of constantly reminding them to practice. Additionally, these challenges help students build the necessary skills through repeated practice, all while having fun and working towards specific goals.

The Geometric Method

At Guitar Ninjas, we use a geometric method that differs from traditional linear approaches. Instead of solely focusing on one area of playing while neglecting others, we categorize guitar playing into 7 key areas: Lead, Rhythm, Fretboard Knowledge, Creativity, Repertoire, Music Theory & Musicianship Skills. Our belief is that students should work on all 7 areas simultaneously to develop comprehensive skills and knowledge across the board.

In the original version of Little Ninjas, we aimed to create the most comprehensive method ever for young learners. While it did offer a high level of comprehensiveness, it was found to be too detailed for the average hobby player, which made the learning process more complicated.

After careful consideration and feedback, we have made adjustments to our approach. We have narrowed our focus and chosen a select number of skills to delve deeper into. This ensures that our curriculum is more streamlined and easier for our young students to learn and follow.

For The Parents: A Note On Expectations

At Guitar Ninjas, we have developed an approach to guitar playing that is attainable for most young learners. Similar to how children read books with lots of pictures and simple sentences, we focus on learning and playing easy music that gradually becomes more complex as they progress.

It's important to understand that learning to play the guitar (or any instrument) proficiently is a long-term commitment that takes years to master. While your child spends several hours each day at school learning subjects like Mathematics and English for 10-12 years, it's statistically likely that they'll only have average performance in these subjects (and may even require additional tutoring in order to excel).

Similarly, with guitar lessons typically being once a week for 30 minutes, it's important to realize that progress may take time. We recommend attending lessons at least twice a week and giving your children 2-3 years to feel comfortable with playing the guitar just to get a hold of the basics.

Children may face challenges and may feel like giving up along their guitar-playing journey. It's crucial to reinforce at home the idea that worthwhile endeavors require time and effort, and that skill is the result of years of practice. When the topic of quitting arises (as it often does), it's important to encourage your child to persevere and determine whether they genuinely don't enjoy it or if they're finding it challenging and trying to avoid it. (Remember, kids are averse to hard work and things that don't come easily)

If you are considering discontinuing your child's lessons, we ask that you evaluate their progress not solely based on their individual achievements (although they will progress at least 4 times faster with Guitar Ninjas compared to standard guitar lessons), but rather on their enthusiasm for guitar and how much they enjoy attending lessons. We believe that fostering a love for music and cultivating a positive attitude towards learning is crucial for their overall development as guitar players.

Thank you for your support as we guide your child through their guitar learning journey at Guitar Ninjas!

A Note On Expectations

We understand the importance of progress, and our Little Ninjas method aims to strike a balance between enjoyment and results. However, we often unfairly compare our progress to the top 1% of professional musicians we hear on CDs and the radio, instead of considering the progress of the average person.

Think about it this way: Would you withdraw your child from football training just because they didn't score 10 goals and make 5 score assists like the best football or basketball players? No, you would encourage them to play the game, have fun, and witness their skills develop over time.

The same mindset is crucial when it comes to music lessons. Our goal is to cultivate a love for music in our students now so that they become self-motivated to practice as they grow older. If we are too strict and demanding when they are young, we risk turning them off from music lessons for life.

Every day, I encounter adult students who wish they had continued with guitar lessons when they were kids and never given up the first time around. Since starting lessons again as adults, none of them have ever expressed regret about getting back into playing the guitar again.

Right now, you have the opportunity to make a positive impact on your child's life and provide them with a lifelong skill that will enhance both of your lives with music.

Let's remember that our children are still developing their language and fine motor skills, as well as their ability to count, communicate, and comprehend. They need our full support for as long as it takes for them to become confident musicians.

So, let's encourage their progress, celebrate their achievements, and foster their love for music, even if it takes time for them to reach their full potential.

The Success Formula For Guitar

To excel at guitar playing, you only need to focus on three things:

1) Attend your weekly lessons consistently.
2) Practice regularly at home.
3) Never give up!

By following these three steps, you have a 100% guarantee of becoming a skilled guitar player. Stay committed and let time work its magic!

Remember, practice makes progress!

"It takes time to be a success, but time is all it takes"

Key Concept 1: The Ladder

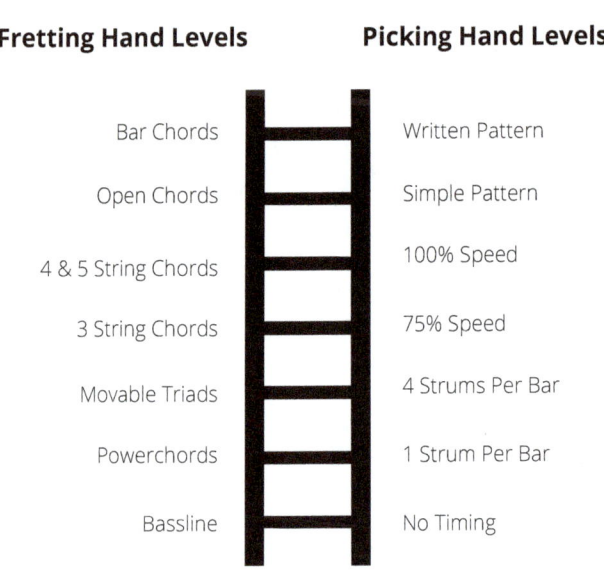

Fretting Hand Levels		Picking Hand Levels
Bar Chords		Written Pattern
Open Chords		Simple Pattern
4 & 5 String Chords		100% Speed
3 String Chords		75% Speed
Movable Triads		4 Strums Per Bar
Powerchords		1 Strum Per Bar
Bassline		No Timing

Imagine going to the gym and attempting to lift a 100kg weight in your first workout. It would likely result in failure.

Unfortunately, many guitar teachers make a similar mistake when they introduce Open Chords to their students in the early lessons. These chords are often too difficult for beginners and especially challenging for young learners (with small hands) who are still developing their fine motor skills.

Many teachers are unaware of the concept of **Levelling & Layering** where any skill, technique, or concept can be broken down into simpler steps. These steps serve as the foundation for what we consider "standard chords."

Instead of setting our students up for failure by pushing them to play something beyond their physical capabilities, we will create more attainable levels for them to work on. This approach ensures that they have fun because the tasks are easier, and it fosters a sense of accomplishment and confidence in their ability to learn guitar.

The ladder diagram above illustrates the levels for both the picking and strumming hands, highlighting that numerous levels precede the introduction of Open Chords and Bar Chords, which are traditionally taught at the beginning.

By following this ladder approach, our students can progress gradually and enjoy their guitar learning journey while building a solid foundation of skill.

Key Concept 2: The Lego Block Practice Method

We have a special saying: "*Say it three times and play it three times*" that helps us learn music quickly and memorise our notes faster.

This saying can be expanded into what we call the **Lego Block Practice Method**.

In this method, we break down the information we want to learn into smaller blocks and gradually piece them together until we have mastered the entire song.

Here's how it works:

1. Say the first chunk of music three times, then play it three times.
2. Say the second chunk of music three times, then play it three times.
3. Combine the first and second chunks into a bigger chunk, say it, and play it three times.
4. Learn the third chunk of music by saying it and playing it three times.
5. Learn the fourth chunk of music by saying it and playing it three times.
6. Combine the third and fourth chunks into a bigger chunk, say it, and play it three times.
7. Finally, put all four chunks together and say and play the entire line of music three times.

If the piece is longer than one line, we simply repeat the process with the new line of music, gradually building the entire piece block by block... just like Lego!

By using this Lego Block Method, we can effectively learn and piece together music, enhancing our overall understanding and retention.

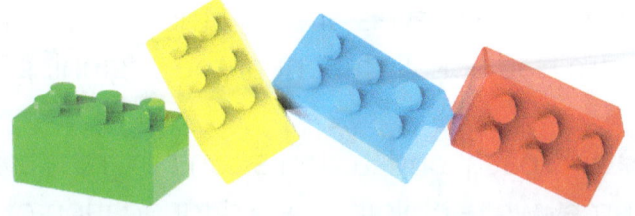

Section 1

Getting Into Guitar

In this chapter you will be learning all of the fundamental skills and concepts you need to play guitar.

Once you have completed this chapter you will be given your White Belt!

How To Pick

Today, we're going to learn a super important skill: how to pick the strings on your guitar!

To do this, you'll need a special tool called a **guitar pick** or **plectrum**. It's a small, teardrop-shaped piece of plastic that helps you make a sound on the guitar. If you don't have a guitar pick, you can also use the bottom edge of your thumb.

Here Is How To Pick

1. Hold the guitar pick between your thumb and first finger, (see the image below)
2. Point the pick back towards the guitar.
3. Bring the pick to the first string, right over the middle of the sound hole.
4. Pluck the string with a small, quick downward motion from your wrist, like this.
5. Let the string ring out for a few seconds, so you can hear the sound it makes.
6. Now, let's repeat this 10 times on the first string, which is the thinnest string.
7. Repeat the same motion 10 times on each of the 6 strings.

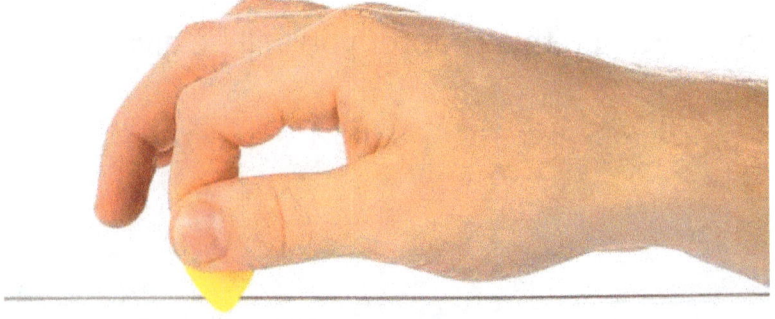

Tip: Remember, when you're picking, make sure to grip the pick firmly in the middle and use the same amount of movement as if you were moving a computer mouse about 2cm on the screen.

How To Fret Notes

In this lesson you will learn the second fundamental skill: How to fret notes.

A fret is a small metal bar embedded within the neck of the guitar. Putting your finger down behind a fret and squeezing shortens the length of the string and changes the sound that you hear. Think of each fret on the guitar like a key on a piano. The lower the fret, the lower the note, the higher the fret the higher the note.

How To Fret Notes

1. Hold your fretting hand as if you had an imaginary can of drink in it.
2. Rotate your hand so your thumb is pointing up towards the roof.
3. Place your thumb in the middle of the neck where the spine would be.
4. Curve your finger and bring the tip down right up near the edge of the first fret of the first string.
5. Squeeze hard enough to make the string press against the wood
6. pluck the string with your picking hand and let it ring out for several seconds.
7. Now move to the 2nd fret and pick it, then the 3rd fret etc.
8. Play all the way to Fret 12 and back again!

Ex 1. How To Fret - Close To The Fret

Ex 2. How Not To Fret - In The Middle Of Two Frets

Tip: Be as close to the fret as you can get without actually touching it. Don't go on top of the fret, and don't be in the middle between two frets.

Tuning The Guitar

Having your guitar in tune will be very important whether you play on your own or with other people.

To tune a guitar all you need to do is pick the string and then turn the tuning peg that matches that string.

Now in order for the guitar to be in tune, each string has to match a particular pitch.

I like to say the phrase **E**aster **B**unnies **G**o **D**ancing **A**t **E**aster.

The first letter of each word becomes the name of the string, and the note we need to tune to.

- The first string is tuned to an E note (thinnest string)
- The second string is tuned to a B note
- The third string is tuned to an G note
- The fourth string is tuned to a D note
- The fifth string is tuned to an A note
- The sixth string is also tuned to an E note. (thickest string)

Most tuners these days will simply give you the name of the string you are playing and tell you whether you are sharp or flat.

If you are really out of tune, you may need to give the string a big twist in order to put it back into the right range for the tuner to pick up.

EG. If you are tuning the E string but your tuner is showing you a B note, you need to tighten the string so it goes from B to C to D and then to E.

Tip: Watch the video on *How To Tune Your Guitar* in your Guitar Dojo Online Account

Reading Guitar Music

In this lesson you will learn how to read guitar music.

As guitarists we are lucky to have our own system of music notation called Guitar Tablature (or TAB for short). Guitar Tablature is a system of lines and numbers that correspond to our strings and the frets we need to play. Although reading standard music notation is a very important skill as beginners we want to start playing and having fun RIGHT NOW and can come back and learn to read music once we already know how to play.

Understanding Tablature

First you need to visualise the fretboard as if the guitar was laid out on a table in front of you with the thin string on top and the thick string on the bottom

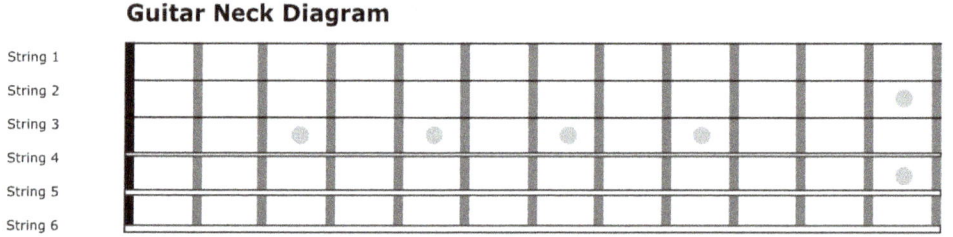

Secondly, you need to reduce the diagram to only include the 6 horizontal lines which represent the strings. Remember: Thin on top, thick on bottom.

Try to first read, and then play the following examples:

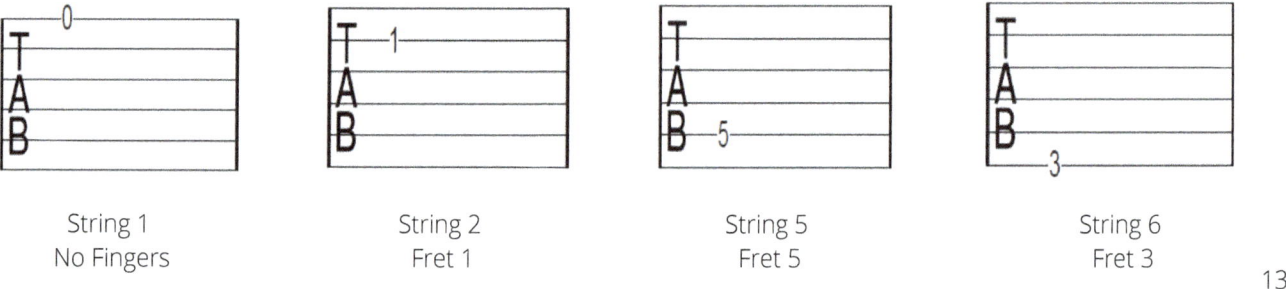

String 1	String 2	String 5	String 6
No Fingers	Fret 1	Fret 5	Fret 3

Notes Along The First String

In this lesson, you will learn the notes along the first string and how to play them using the picking technique.

The first example below is the E Natural Minor scale. We'll outline the best way to learn and practice it below:

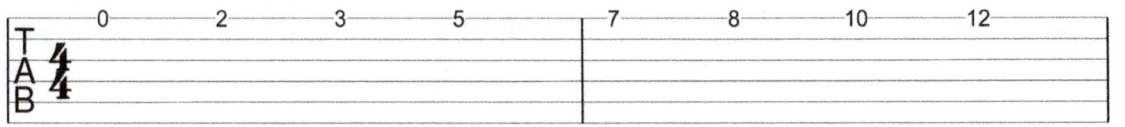

1. Say the first four numbers out loud three times.
2. Play the first four number three times.
3. Say the second four numbers out loud three times.
4. Play the second four number three times.
5. Say all eight numbers out loud three times.
6. Play all eight numbers three times

We call this the **Say It Three Times, Play It Three Times** method. We have found that it is the best way to help you learn and memorise new information and to help you retain it long term. In the case of longer pieces of music you should do each indiviudal line of music three times each before putting the entire piece together.

Once you have learned a piece of music we recommend you try to play it in new ways to reinforce what you know and keep practice fun and exciting with some additional challenges. Try some of the following:

- Playing it Backwards (from 12 to 0)
- Playing it 10 Times In A Row without any mistakes.
- Playing it using only Upstrokes.
- Playing it while Standing Up.
- Playing it with your Eyes Shut.

How many of the challenges above can you do?

Strumming

In this lesson you will reinforce the E Natural Minor Scale you learned previously while also integrating it with a new technique called **Strumming**.

Strumming is when you play two or more strings at the same time using one single motion. Use the same motion as if you had just washed your hands and were flicking the water off.

We can identify strumming in Guitar Tab when the numbers are stacked up on top of each other like the examples below:

In the first example you can see three 0's stacked up on top of each other, this means they need to be played at the same time using the strum technique. In the second example we are fretting the 2nd fret of string 1 but still strumming the 2nd and 3rd string openly. Try playing the example below.

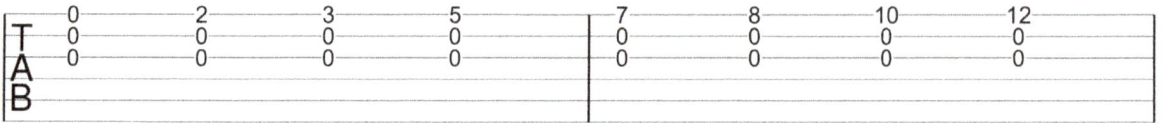

Hopefully you noticed that it was the same E Natural Minor Scale you learned in the previous lesson, but this time you are using strumming to include other strings. You should still:

- Play it forwards three times.
- Play it backwards three times.
- Play it 10 times in a row without any mistakes.
- Play it while standing up.
- Play it with your eyes shut.

Picking Patterns

In this lesson you will you will learn how to combine your E Natural Minor scale with picking patterns to create beautiful sounds on the guitar.

A **Picking Pattern** is simply a sequential order that you pick individual strings in that is repeated across one or several bars of music. Below is an example of what a picking pattern looks like in Guitar Tab

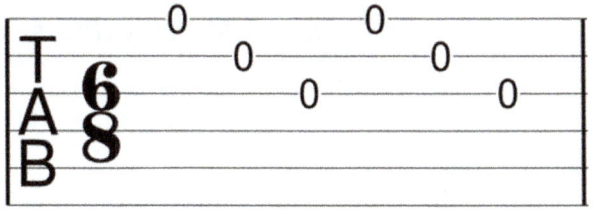

Unlike strumming where the numbers are stacked upon each other. We can see that we are still playing on multiple strings but individually in the order of the first string, then second, then third. Play this pattern 10-20 times until you can do it smoothly.

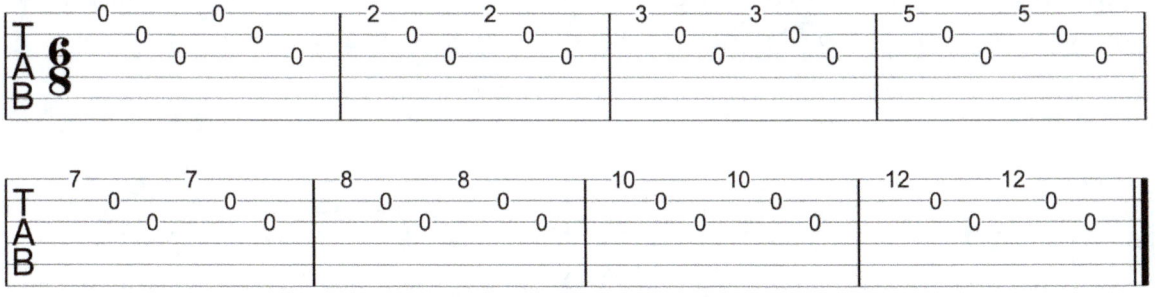

In the example above we are still playing our E natural minor scale, but are now applying a 6 note picking pattern to each note.

- Play the pattern twice on the open strings
- Move your first finger to the 2nd fret on string one and play the same picking pattern.
- Keep moving along each note of the scale until you get to fret 12.
- Repeat this three times.

Congratulations! You have now learned all of your fundamental skills!

Picking Study

Here is a short study piece that uses our picking skill along the first string. This piece will reinforce your picking and fretting technique, and introduce you to learning larger pieces of music.

How to learn this piece.

- Say the first line three times, then play it three times.
- Say the second line three times, then play it three times.
- Say the third line three times, then play it three times.
- Say the fourth line three times, then play it three times.
- Now play from the start of the piece to the end of the piece three times.

When you practice this way you are training your brain to remember the numbers and not be reliant on reading every single note. This will result in more of your attention going towards your fingers and making sure they are doing the correct motions which will result in fewer mistakes and cleaner playing.

Of course you can look up at the music for guidance whenever you need to.

Strumming Study

Here is a short study piece that uses our strumming skill combined with notes along the first string.

How to Learn this Piece.

- Say the first line three times, then play it three times.
- Say the second line three times, then play it three times.
- Say the third line three times, then play it three times.
- Say the fourth line three times, then play it three times.
- Now play from the start of the piece to the end of the piece three times

Other Tips

Remember to let the notes ring out for four counts after each strum before you move onto the next note.

Be mindful that your pick doesn't come to rest on the third string in anticipation of your strum, this will mute the string.

Picking Pattern Study

Here is a short study piece that uses picking patterns along with notes on the first string.

Often the biggest challenge people have with picking pattern pieces is remembering the patterns and having to look between their hands each time they change string.

A great exercise to help overcome this is to focus on playing the pattern with your eyes shut. Play the pattern 3 times with your eyes open, then 3 times with your eyes shut. Open your eyes and play it another three times and then shut your eyes and try to get 5 times with your eyes shut. Open your eyes for 3 more times before trying to go 10 times in a row with your eyes shut. if you can do this, you won't need to look at your picking hand anymore.

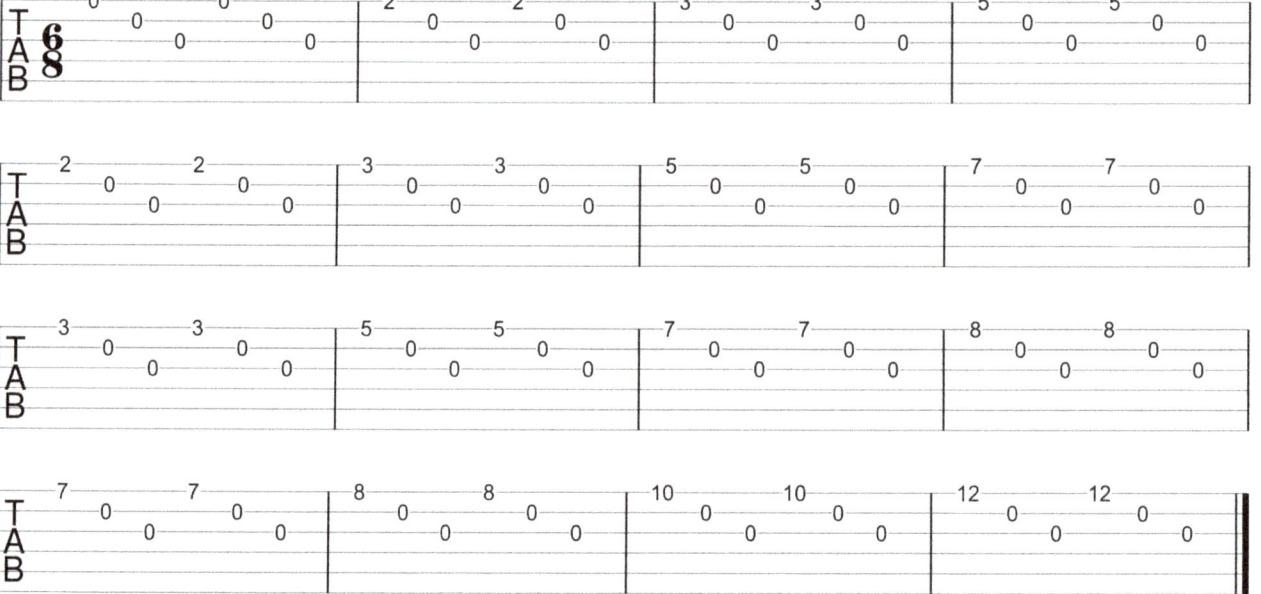

How to learn this piece.

- Say the first line three times, then play it three times.
- Say the second line three times, then play it three times.
- Say the third line three times, then play it three times.
- Say the fourth line three times, then play it three times.
- Now play from the start of the piece to the end of the piece three times.

The Major Scale

Earlier in this book you learned 8 notes along string number 1.

While you didn't know it at the time, you learned your very first scale - The Natural Minor Scale!

In this lesson, you will learn the Major Scale which is the foundation of all Western Music.

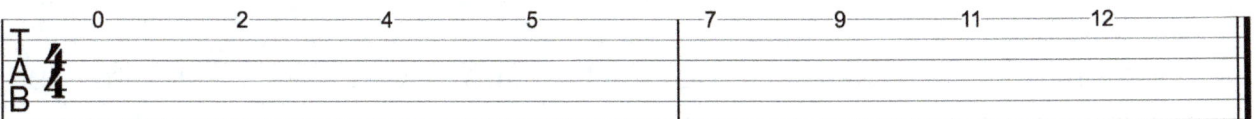

Use the **Say It Three Times, Play It Three Times** method to learn and practice the Major Scale along on string 1. Notice how it sounds and feels different to the minor scale you learned previously.

Major Scale Study Piece

Once you have learned the major scale above you can put it into practice with a brand-new study piece composed in the Key of E Major on string 1. Note that this piece uses several different rhythms so pay attention to which notes ring out for longer.

Tip: The pieces from here on will get longer and more challenging. To make learning easier break each line into individual bars, learn each bar separately and then put them together before moving on to the next line.

Skipping Notes

Our next study piece will continue to use the E Major Scale on String 1.

This time we will be skipping notes in order to challenge your ability to change between notes smoothly.

You may wish to work on switching between two individual notes in isolation several times until it becomes smooth before you move on to the next notes.

This means that the 8 notes in the first line could be divided up into 4 chunks of two notes each, then two chunks of four notes, before putting the entire line together.

How to learn this piece.

- Say and play the first two notes three times each.
- Say and play the next two notes three times each.
- Say and play all four notes in the first bar three times each.
- Repeat steps 1-3 for the second bar on the first line.
- Put the entire first line together and play it three times.
- Repeat this process for all four lines before putting the entire piece together

Changing Direction

For this piece, we are returning to our Natural Minor Scale on String 1 which uses the notes 0 2 3 5 7 8 10 12.

We will be using a combination of note rhythms while playing melodies that ascend (go from low notes to high notes) and descend (high to low) in different directions.

Once again, learn the piece bar by bar before putting it all together.

Additional Levels

Try some of these additional levels to make the piece more challenging.

- Play the song as written on a single string
- Try playing the same notes but on a different string
- Try strumming the longer notes (include strings 2 & 3)
- Try strumming every note
- Try adding your own picking pattern to the piece
- Convert the piece from E Minor to E Major by changing the 3's to 4's and the 8's to 9's.

Six String Picking Pattern

Our final Study Piece includes the 6th string in the picking pattern and will sound a lot fuller as all the notes resonate with each other.

It's important to practice the picking pattern in isolation before attempting to apply it to the rest of the piece.

Remember, just say the number that changes in each bar (0 2 3 5, 7 5 8 7 etc) and apply the picking pattern.

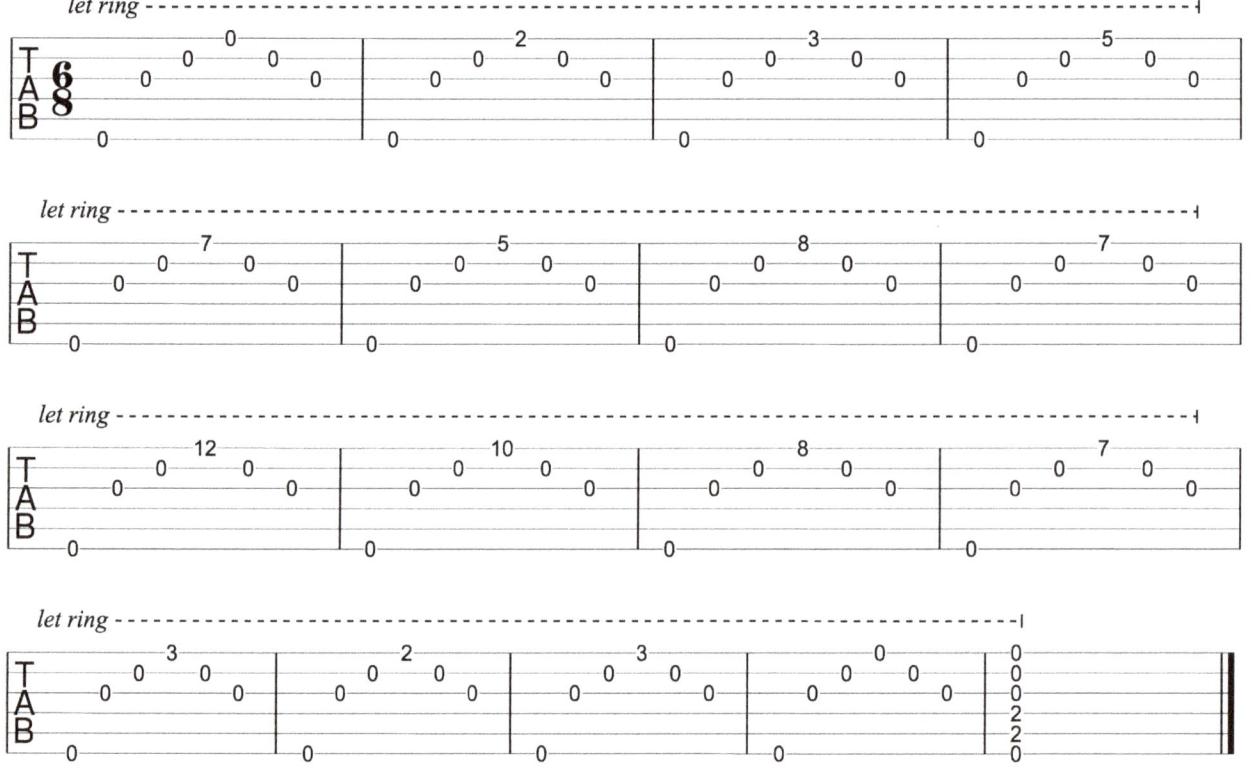

How To Learn This Piece

- Practice the picking pattern (6 3 2 1 2 3) in isolation until you can play it smoothly without mistakes
- Apply the picking pattern to the first four numbers (0 2 3 5) three times.
- Apply the picking pattern to the next four numbers (7 5 8 7) three times.
- Apply the picking pattern to the next four numbers (12 10 8 7) three times.
- Apply the picking pattern to the last four numbers (3 2 3 0) three times.
- Put it all together and finish with an Em chord strummed on all 6 strings.

What Next?

Congratulations! You have completed your Getting Into Guitar Training and have now earned your White Belt!

Moving forward this book is divided into 5 sections, each corresponding to a key area of guitar playing in our geometric learning model. Each section contains exercises and challenges that you need to complete in order to level up and progress through the Little Ninjas system. We have designed it this way for two important reasons:

1. It's fun to complete challenges, earn experience points, and level up! You'll enjoy the sense of accomplishment as you advance.
2. The challenges are designed to help you practice with specific goals in mind, such as improving your memory, consistency, performing under pressure, and creativity. This makes your practice more focused and effective compared to mindless repetition.

To earn additional Guitar Ninjas Badges make sure you complete all the exercises and challenges for each worksheet within the 6 sections of this book.

As you finish each challenge, mark it off in the provided boxes. After your practice session, count up your marks and fill up the experience meter at the bottom of the page.

Once you have completed all the challenges and filled up your experience meter, you will level up and unlock the next level for that area of guitar playing.

Remember, some challenges may take a few practice sessions to complete, so don't worry if you can't finish everything in one day. Just keep practising and you will improve over time.

You've got this! Good luck on your journey to earning your White Belt and beyond!

Section 2

Warmups

In this section, we're going to start by warming up each hand separately before bringing them together to play scales.

These warmups will help you improve your finger coordination, dexterity, and the connection between your hands and your brain.

Each worksheet will have a few challenges for you to complete, and there will be a checklist to help you keep track of your progress. If you're not sure how to do something, don't hesitate to ask your teacher to explain the challenges or to show you what to do.

Let's get started!

White Belt Warmups

These simple exercises are great warmups that you should spend a minute or two practising every day!

To play each exercise, put your finger on the frets that match the numbers written below. (0 = no fingers, 1 = first finger, 2 = second finger, 3 = third finger and 4 = pinkie finger)

You'll also notice five boxes next to each warmup and five corresponding challenges in the bubbles below. Complete the challenge to earn the tick!

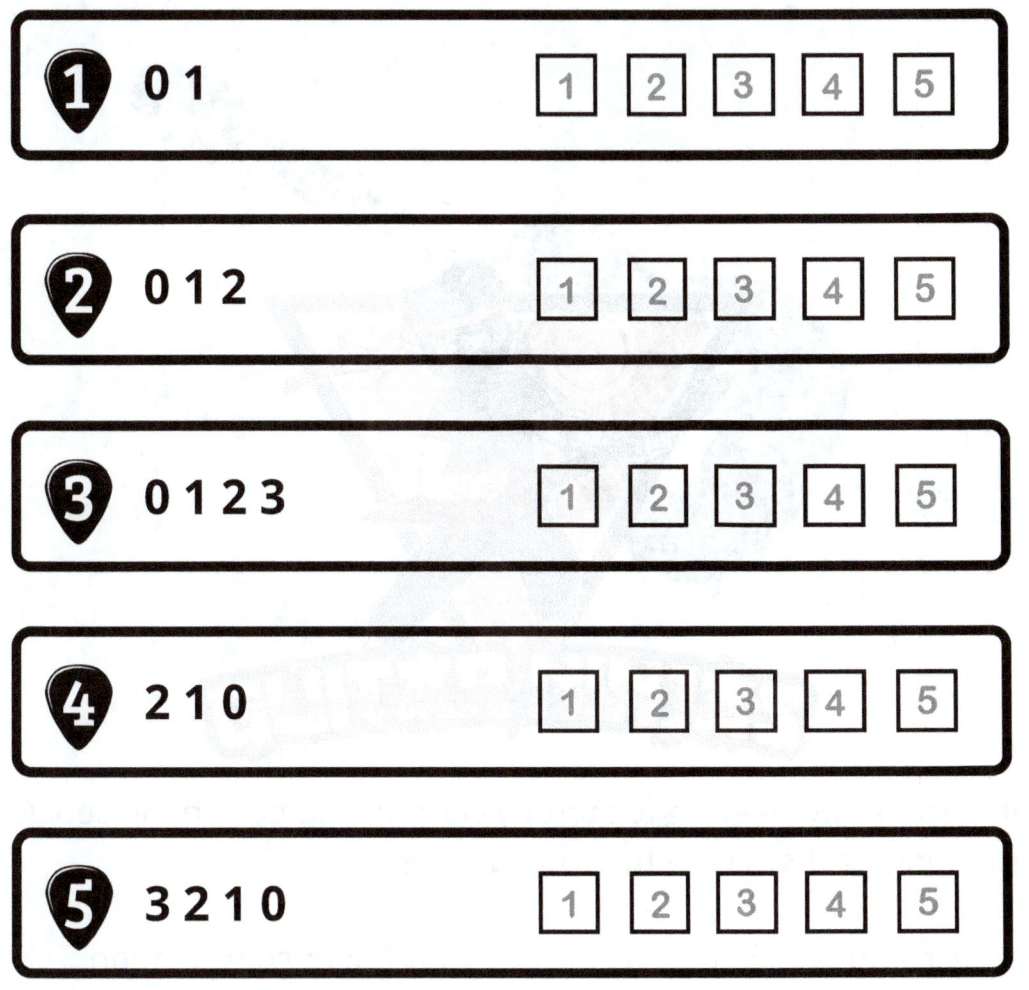

1 0 1   1 2 3 4 5

2 0 1 2   1 2 3 4 5

3 0 1 2 3   1 2 3 4 5

4 2 1 0   1 2 3 4 5

5 3 2 1 0   1 2 3 4 5

Warmup Challenges & Experience Meter

First Playthrough Any Fingers	Three In A Row Correct Fingers	Ten In A Row No Mistakes	Eyes Shut Three In A Row	All 6 String Correct Fingers
5 complete	10 complete	15 complete	20 complete	25 Complete Level Up!

Yellow Belt Warmups

Here are five more warmups to help train your fingers. For these exercises we will be introducing your pinkie finger which is used to play fret 4.

Your pinkie might not want to co-operate at first, but with regular practice it will become as strong as every other finger.

We've also given you five more challenges to try out, make sure you use the right fingers!

Warmup Challenges

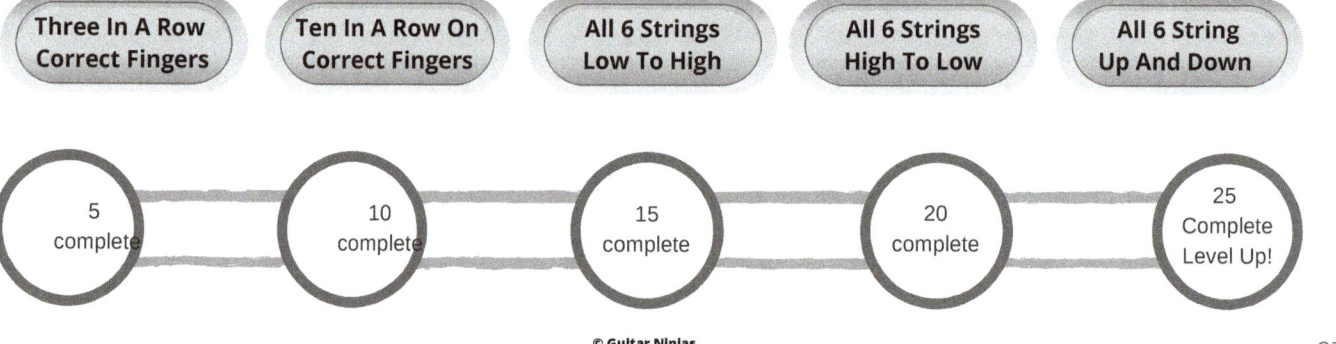

© Guitar Ninjas
Little Ninjas Guitar Method Book
www.GuitarNinjas.com.au

Orange Belt Warmups

Here are five more warmups to help train your fingers. You will be getting to use all four fingers in every one of these exercises.

You might find some of these exercises tricky, remember to go slow at first and built up speed as you get more confident.

Some of the challenges will be slightly different to the ones in previous exercises. We change them up to keep them interesting...and to keep you on your toes!

Warmup Challenges

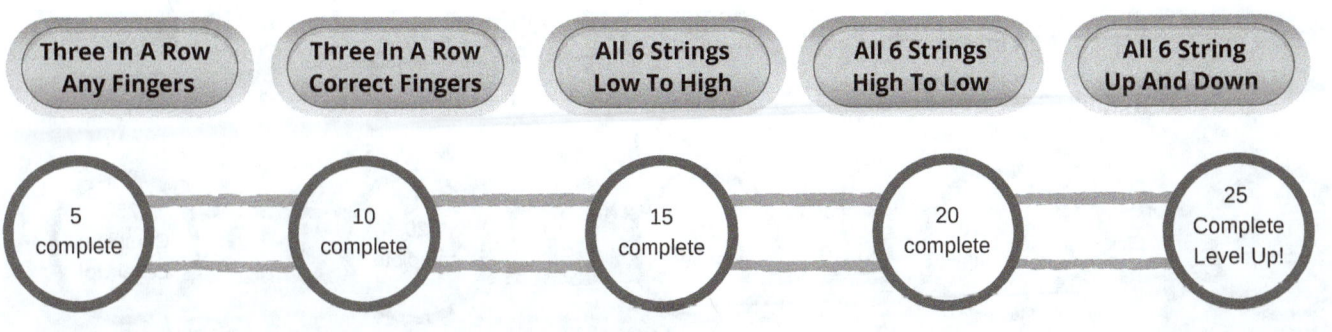

White Belt Picking Hand Warmups

These simple exercises are great for warming up your picking hand and helping you build dexterity.

To play each exercise do 10 picks on the given string(s) following the pattern that you've been given.

You'll also notice the three boxes for each challenge have the letters D, U or A next to them. D = Down Strokes, U = Up Strokes and A = Alternate Picking where pick down, and then up on each string.

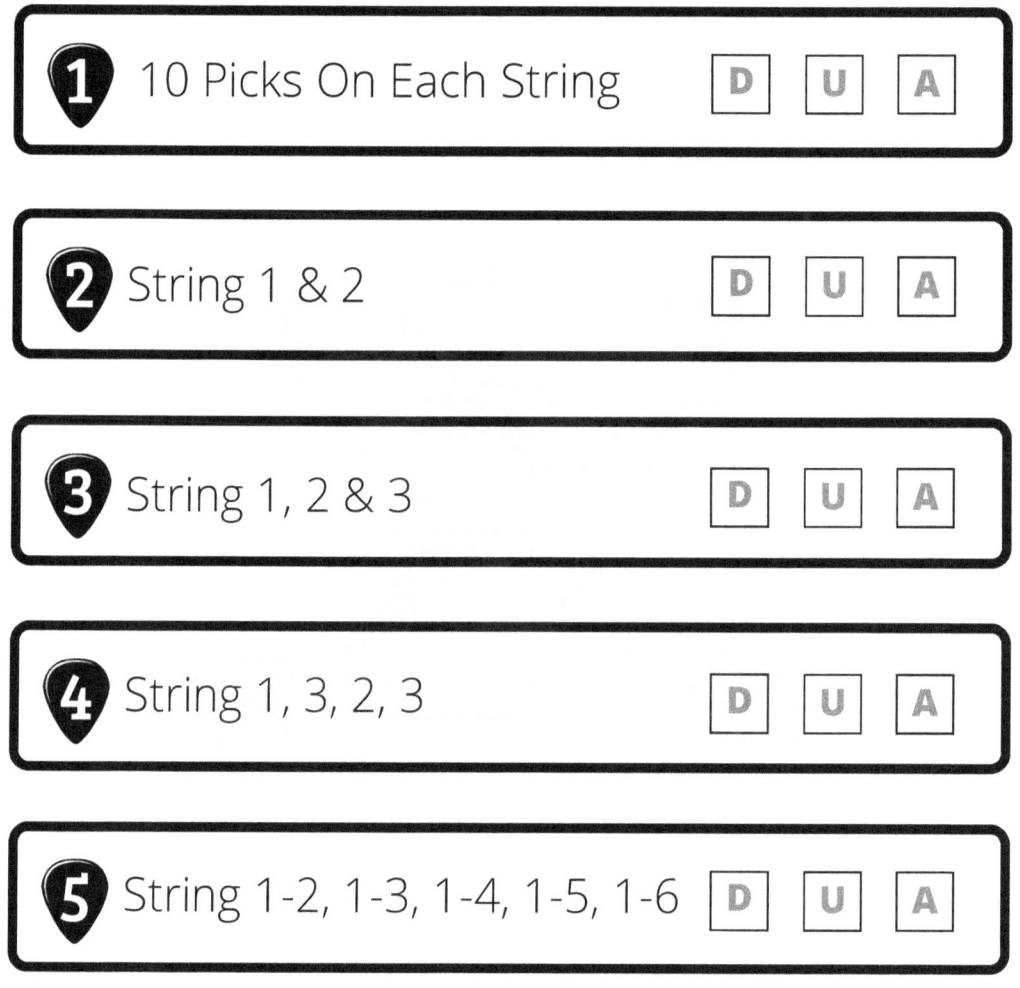

1 10 Picks On Each String — D U A

2 String 1 & 2 — D U A

3 String 1, 2 & 3 — D U A

4 String 1, 3, 2, 3 — D U A

5 String 1-2, 1-3, 1-4, 1-5, 1-6 — D U A

Warmup Challenges & Experience Meter

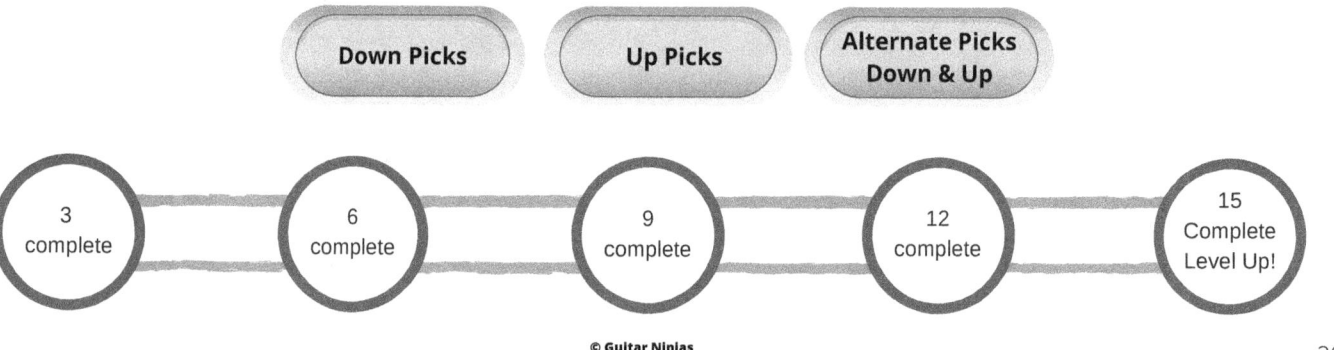

Down Picks — Up Picks — Alternate Picks Down & Up

3 complete — 6 complete — 9 complete — 12 complete — 15 Complete Level Up!

Yellow Belt Picking Hand Warmups

Here are some additional exercises to warm up your picking hand and build more coordination.

To play each exercise do 20 picks on the given string(s) following the pattern that you've been assigned.

You'll also notice the three boxes for each challenge have the letters D, U or A next to them. D = Down Strokes, U = Up Strokes and A = Alternate Picking where you pick down and then up on the string.

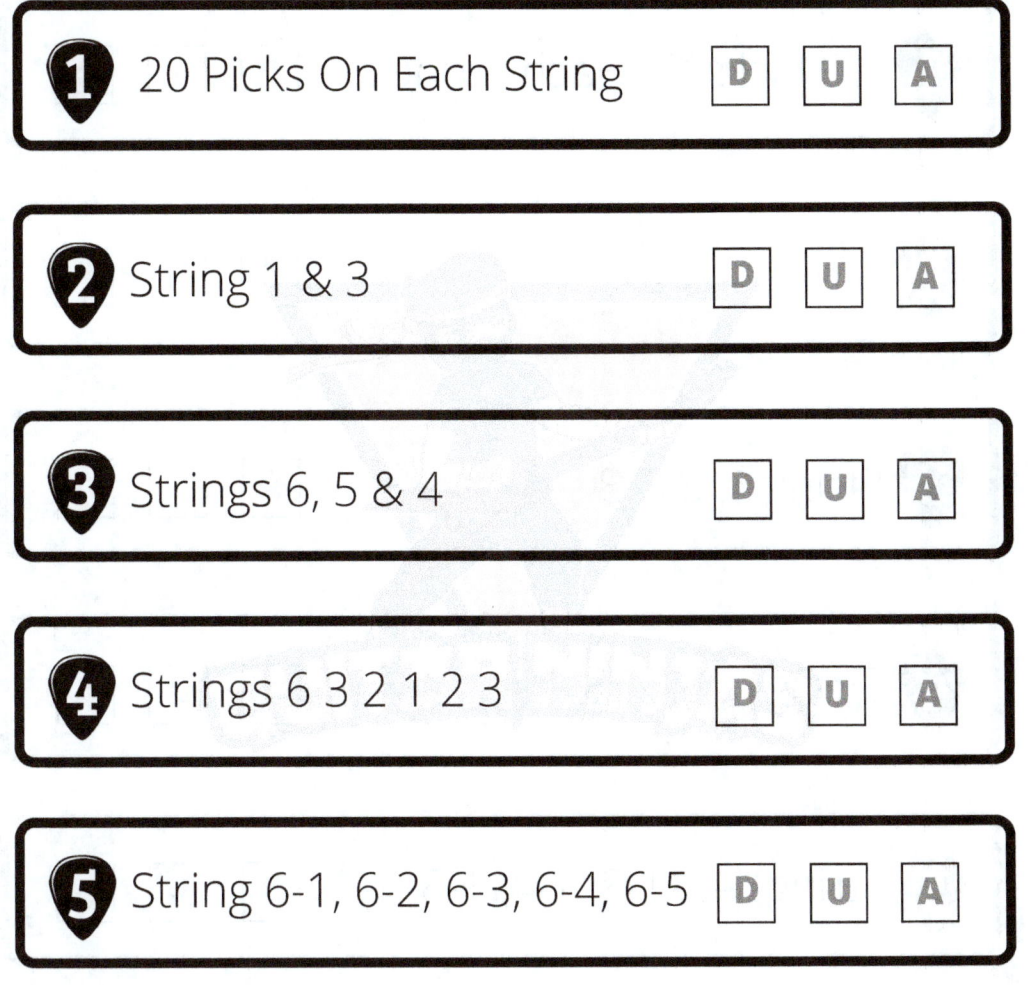

1 20 Picks On Each String   D   U   A

2 String 1 & 3   D   U   A

3 Strings 6, 5 & 4   D   U   A

4 Strings 6 3 2 1 2 3   D   U   A

5 String 6-1, 6-2, 6-3, 6-4, 6-5   D   U   A

Warmup Challenges & Experience Meter

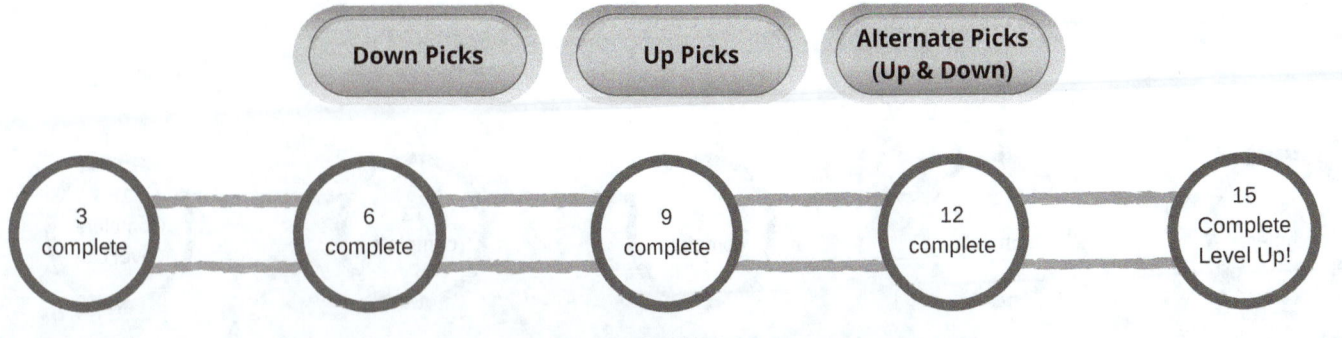

Down Picks   Up Picks   Alternate Picks (Up & Down)

3 complete   6 complete   9 complete   12 complete   15 Complete Level Up!

Orange Belt Picking Hand Warmups

Our final set of picking hand warmup exercises will be even more challenging!

To play each exercise do 10 picks on the given string(s) following the pattern that you've been given.

You'll also notice the three boxes for each challenge have the letters D, U or A next to them. D = Down Strokes, U = Up Strokes and A = Alternate Picking where you do down then up picks.

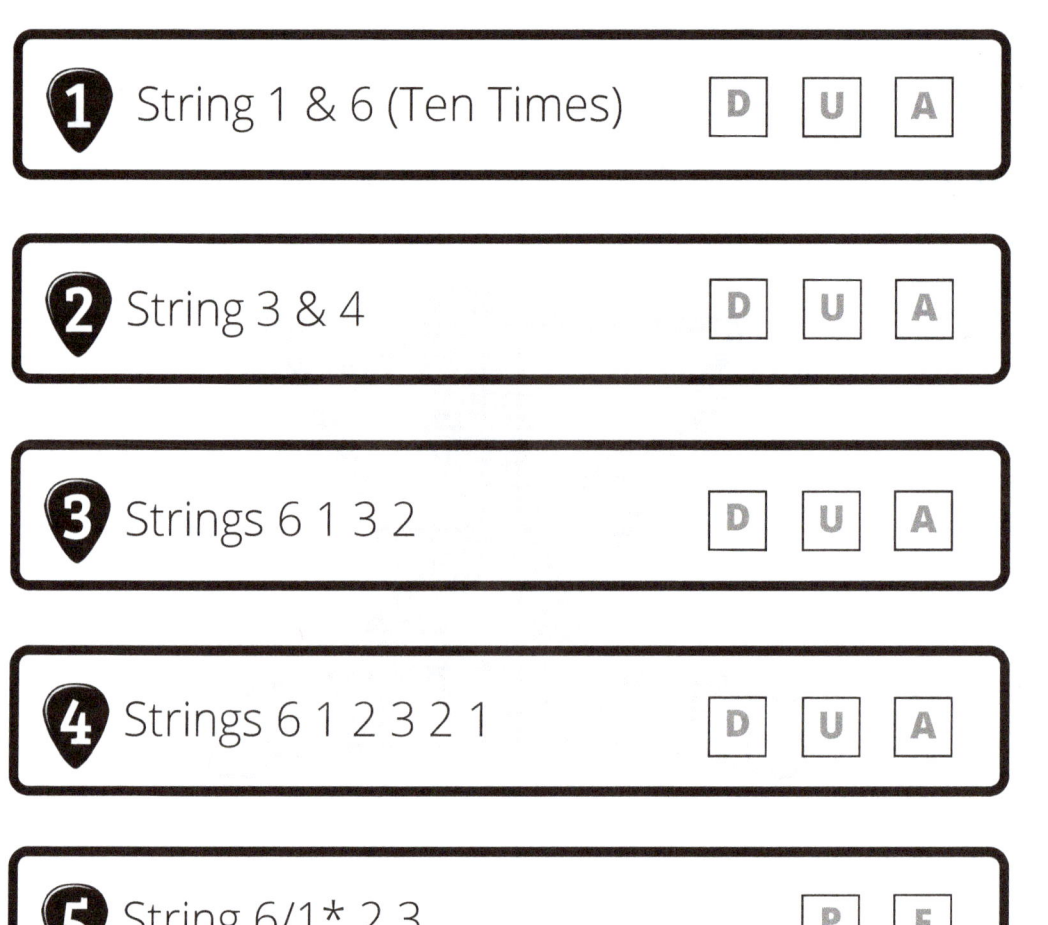

1 String 1 & 6 (Ten Times)   D   U   A

2 String 3 & 4   D   U   A

3 Strings 6 1 3 2   D   U   A

4 Strings 6 1 2 3 2 1   D   U   A

5 String 6/1* 2 3   P   F

*Play string 6 and 1 at the same time with a c combination of pick and fingers, or two different fingers P = Pick, F = Fingers (this is known as hybrid picking)

Warmup Challenges & Experience Meter

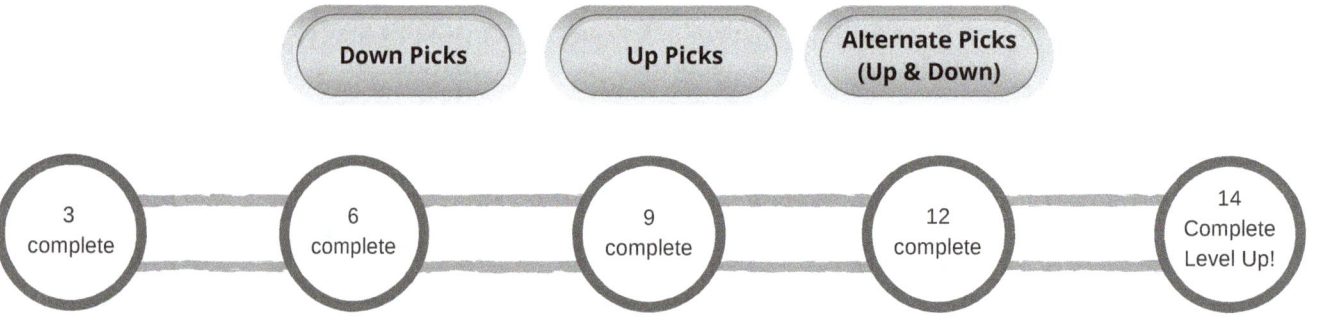

Down Picks   Up Picks   Alternate Picks (Up & Down)

3 complete   6 complete   9 complete   12 complete   14 Complete Level Up!

Little Ninjas Scales

A **Scale** is a collection of notes arranged in a particular pattern. This pattern is known as the **Scale Formula** and is responsible for a scale sounding a particular way. Think of the scale formula as a recipe that you follow to create a specific sound.

Traditionally, scales are played vertically across all 6 strings. We will learn how to play them horizontaly across a single string using only a group of numbers.

Learn scales using the **Say It Three Times, Play It Three Times** method. You may want to break them up into two halves and learn them separatly before putting it all together.

The Major Scale

1 0 2 4 5 7 9 11 12   [1] [2] [3] [4] [5]

The Major Scale has the formula T T S T T T S

The Minor Scale

2 0 2 3 5 7 8 10 12   [1] [2] [3] [4] [5]

The Minor Scale has the formula T S T T S T T

The Major Pentatonic Scale

3 0 2 4 7 9 12   [1] [2] [3] [4] [5]

The Major Pentatonic Scale has the formula T T T.5 T T.5

The Minor Pentatonic Scale

4 0 3 5 8 10 12   [1] [2] [3] [4] [5]

The Minor Pentatonic Scale has the formula T.5 T T T.5 T

The Blues Scale

5 0 3 5 6 7 10 12   [1] [2] [3] [4] [5]

The Blues Scale has the formula T.5 T S S T.5 T

The Harmonic Minor Scale

6 0 2 3 5 7 8 11 12   [1] [2] [3] [4] [5]

The H/M Scale has the formula T S T T S T.5 S

The Whole Tone Scale

7 0 2 4 6 8 10 12   [1] [2] [3] [4] [5]

The Whole Tone Scale has the formula T T T T T T

The Double Harmonic Scale

8 0 1 4 5 7 8 11 12   [1] [2] [3] [4] [5]

The Double Harmonic Scale has the formula S T.5 S T S T.5 S

Scale Challenges & Experience Meter

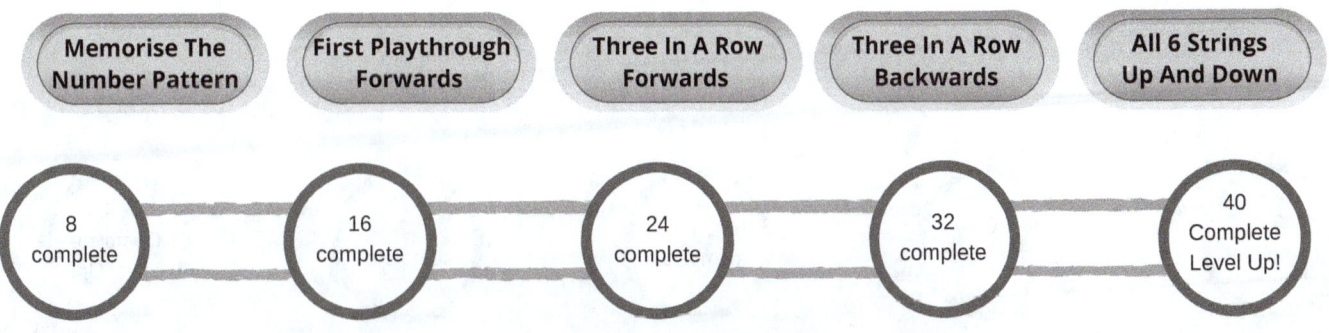

Memorise The Number Pattern | First Playthrough Forwards | Three In A Row Forwards | Three In A Row Backwards | All 6 Strings Up And Down

8 complete — 16 complete — 24 complete — 32 complete — 40 Complete Level Up!

© Guitar Ninjas
Little Ninjas Guitar Method Book
www.GuitarNinjas.com.au

Section 3

Melodies

A melody is a musical idea that is made up of a series of notes.

These notes come from a scale and are put together in a meaningful way to create a musical phrase.

You can think of melodies as the catchy parts of your favourite songs that you like to sing along to.

In our lessons, we'll be exploring 9 different levels of melodies, starting from easy white belt ideas and working our way up to more complex Black Belt level tunes.

It's going to be a fun journey as we learn to create and play our own melodies! Let's get started!

White Belt Melodies

A **Melody** is a short arrangement of notes into a meaningful musical phrase. It can be part of an entire piece or a stand-alone musical idea. Many of your favourite nursery rhymes or sing-along songs are often short little melodies.

We're going to learn a number of melodies in order to train our fingers to effectively play single note lines. It will also be a lot of fun playing songs that our friends and family members know and can sing along to. We've arranged all the melodies in the first few levels so that you can play them on a single string.

We recommend that you learn the melodies using the **say it three times, play it three times** approach. We've also included the lyrics so that you can have a sing along too.

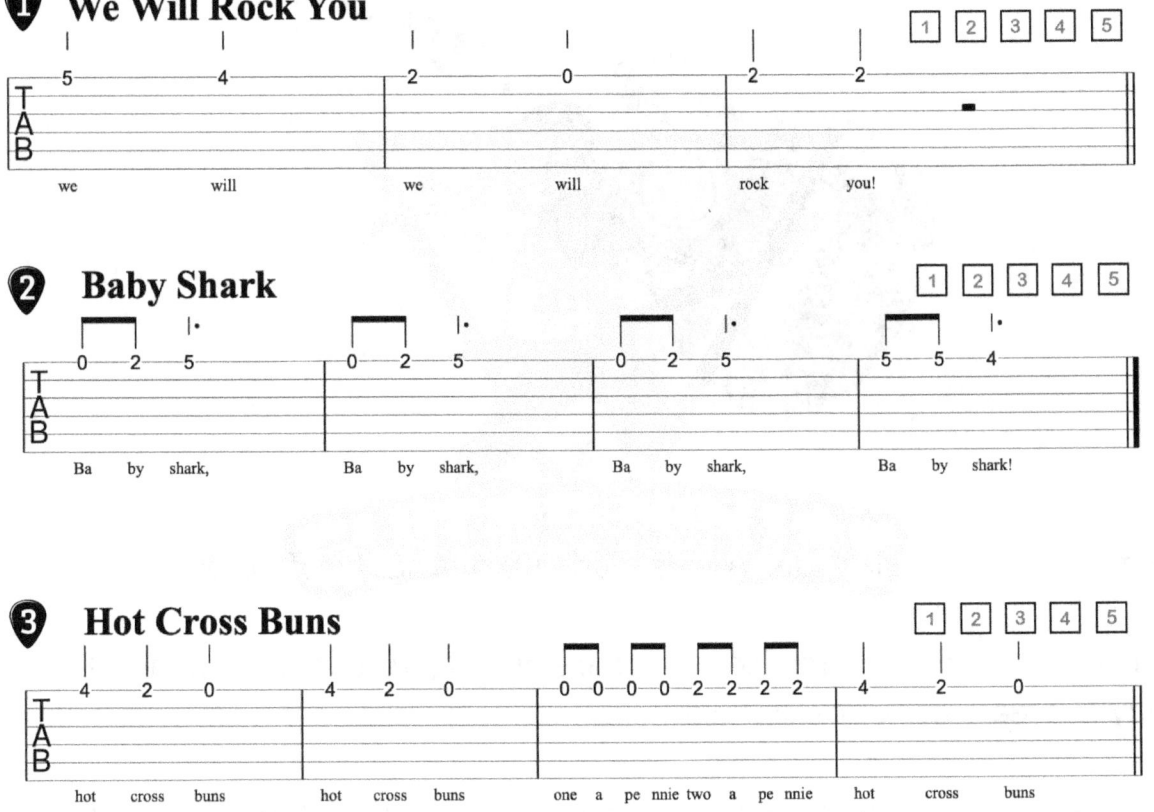

Melody Challenges & Experience Meter

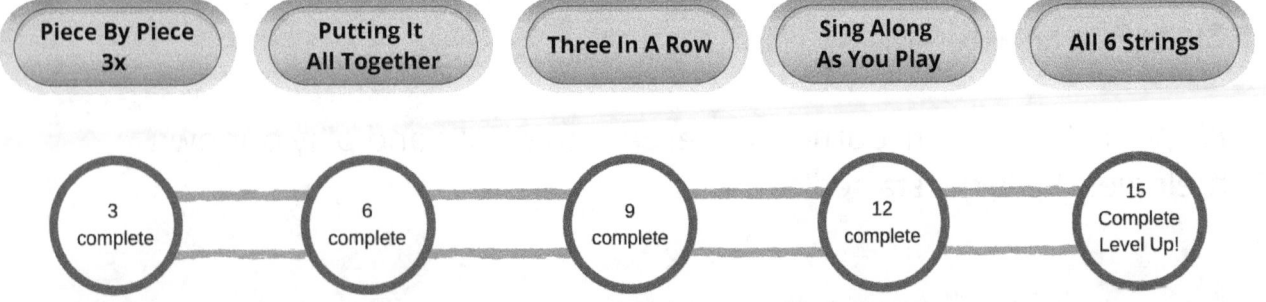

Yellow Belt Melodies

Here are three more melodies to help you improve both your guitar playing and your singing abilities. Notice how one of the three melodies is played on the 2nd string. Can you spot which one it is?

1 Cocomelon

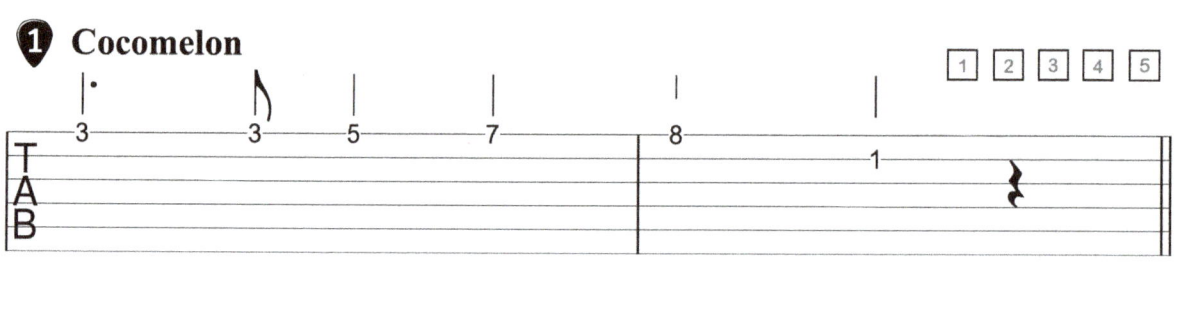

2 I'm Lovin' It

Da   Da   Da   Da   Daa

3 Dynamite

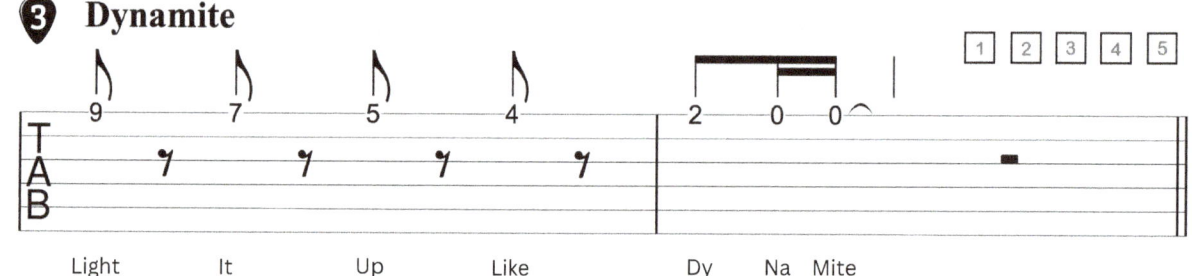

Light   It   Up   Like   Dy   Na   Mite

Remember: The best way to get good at something is to practice it EVERY DAY!

Melody Challenges

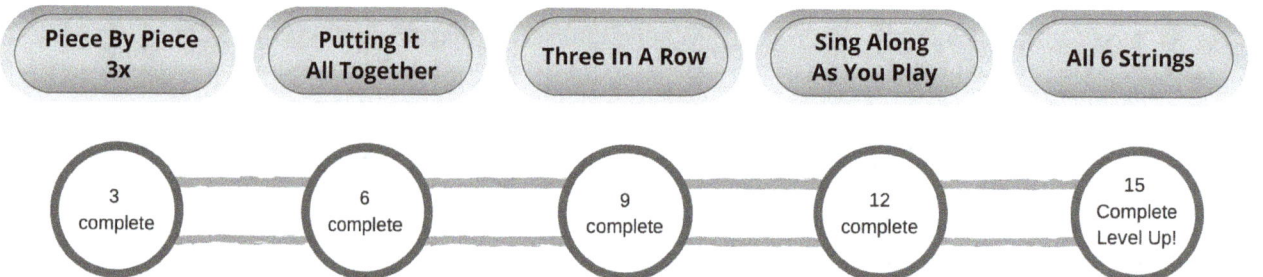

Orange Belt Melodies

Make sure you are singing along to each song as you learn to play it. (If there are no lyrics you can just sing the fret numbers). Connecting your voice to the notes on the guitar is a great skill to have. If the notes are too high for your voice, try playing the melody on another string.

1 Shape Of You

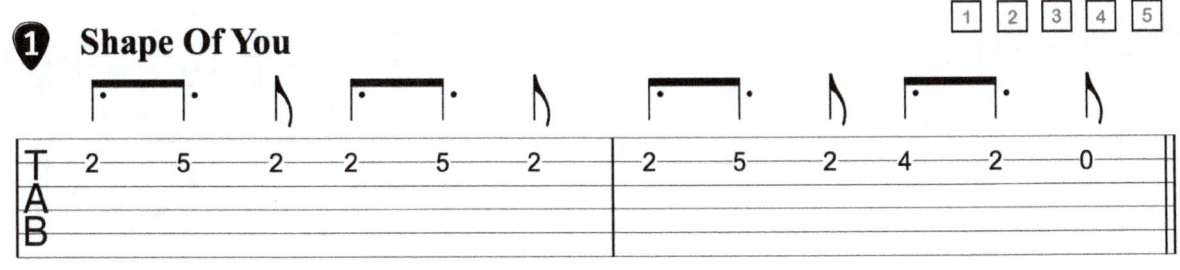

2 Peppa Pig

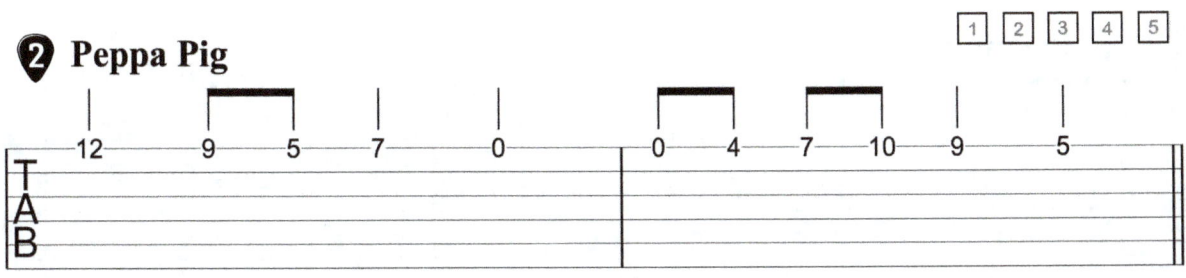

3 Bluey

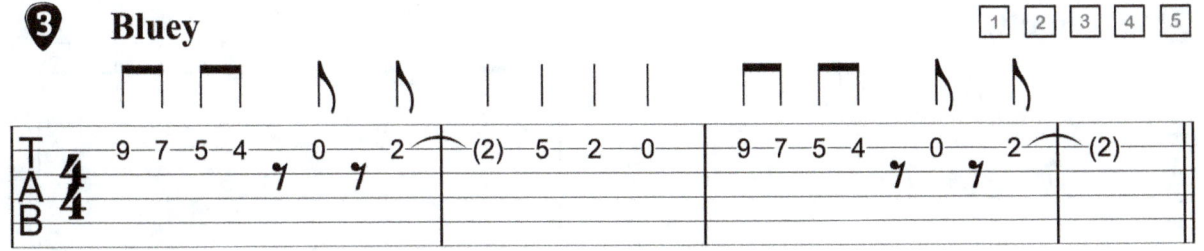

Note: The funny ⅞ symbol in the Bluey riff is an eigth note rest. This indicates silence so try to stop the string ringing out each time you see one of these.

Melody Challenges

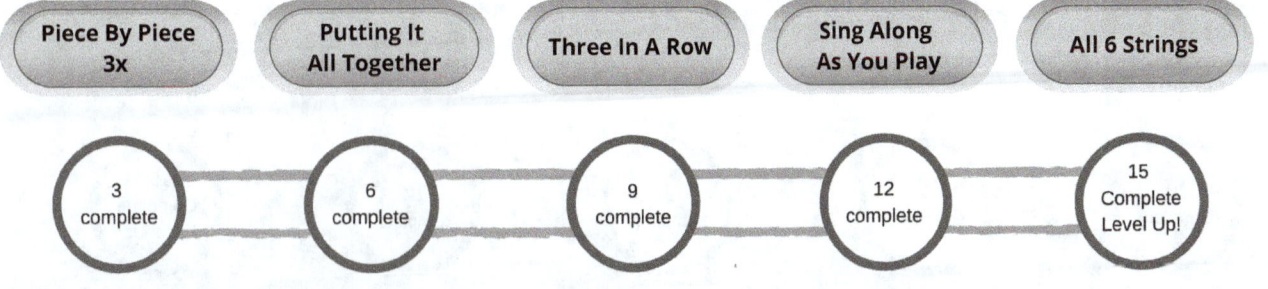

Green Belt Melodies

Here are three more melodies to help you learn. Notice how our first melody is played exclusively on string 2 while the second melody uses both string 1 and string 2.

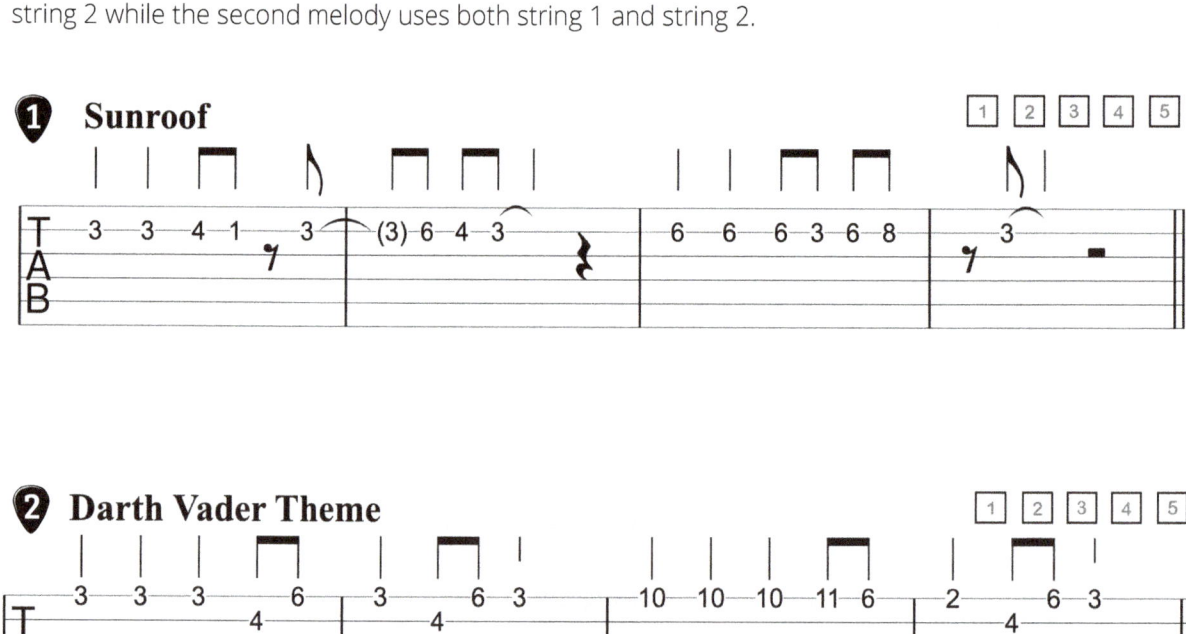

❶ Sunroof

❷ Darth Vader Theme

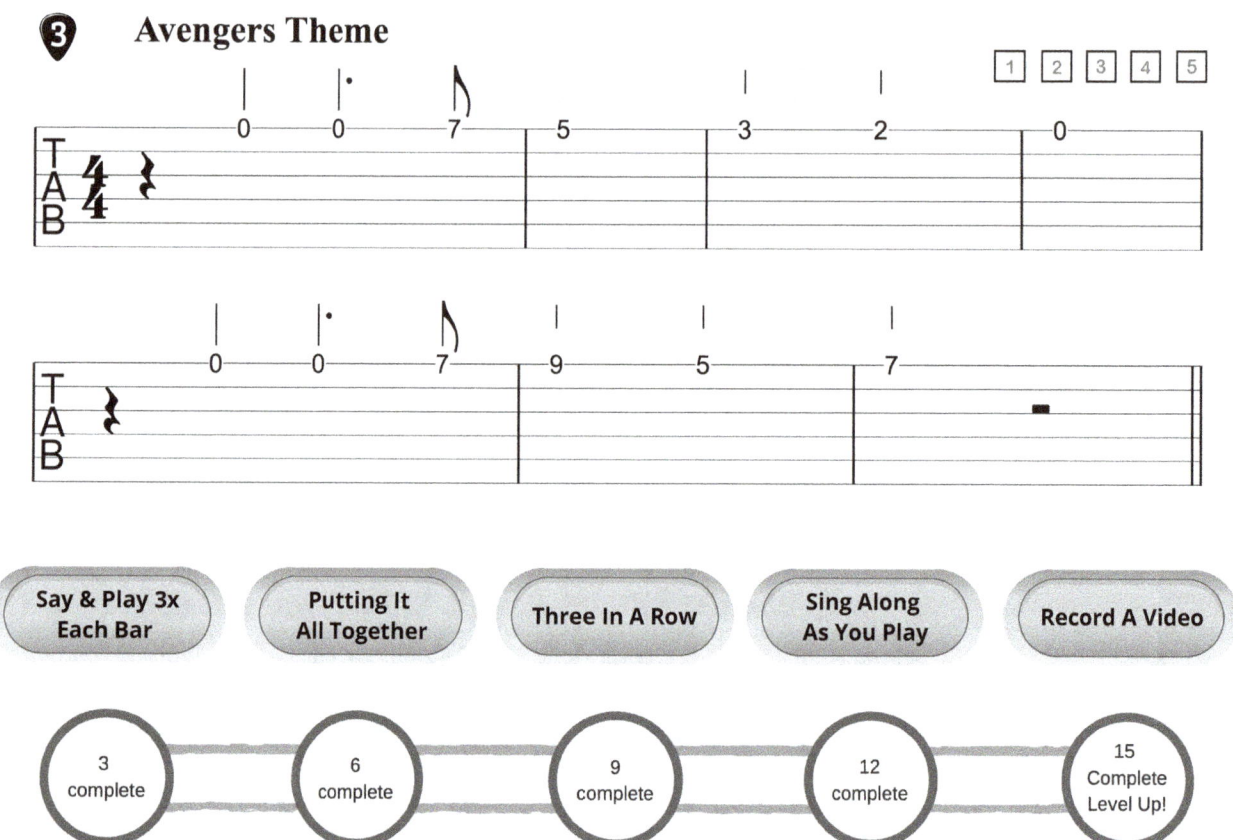

❸ Avengers Theme

| Say & Play 3x Each Bar | Putting It All Together | Three In A Row | Sing Along As You Play | Record A Video |

| 3 complete | 6 complete | 9 complete | 12 complete | 15 Complete Level Up! |

© Guitar Ninjas
Little Ninjas Guitar Method Book
www.GuitarNinjas.com.au

37

Blue Belt Melodies

In the first version of the book most of the melodies we learned very nursery rhymes. We hope that you're recognising and enjoying learning a mix of both contemporary and traditional examples.

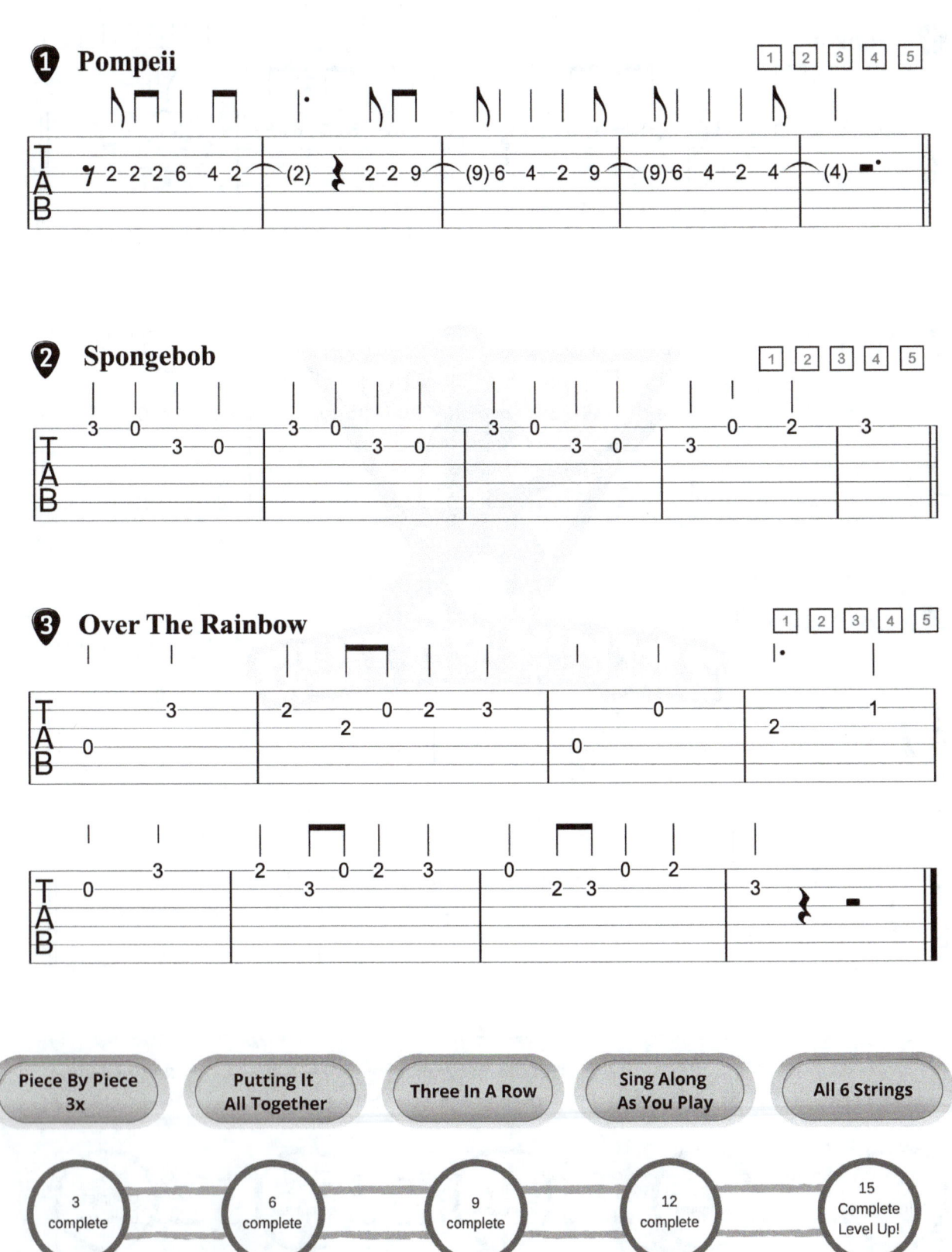

| Piece By Piece 3x | Putting It All Together | Three In A Row | Sing Along As You Play | All 6 Strings |

3 complete — 6 complete — 9 complete — 12 complete — 15 Complete Level Up!

Purple Belt Melodies

As some of these study pieces are getting longer and trickier, we've reduced the number of pieces you need to learn for this level from three to two. If you run out of challenges try using some of the ones from other levels.

1 Star Wars

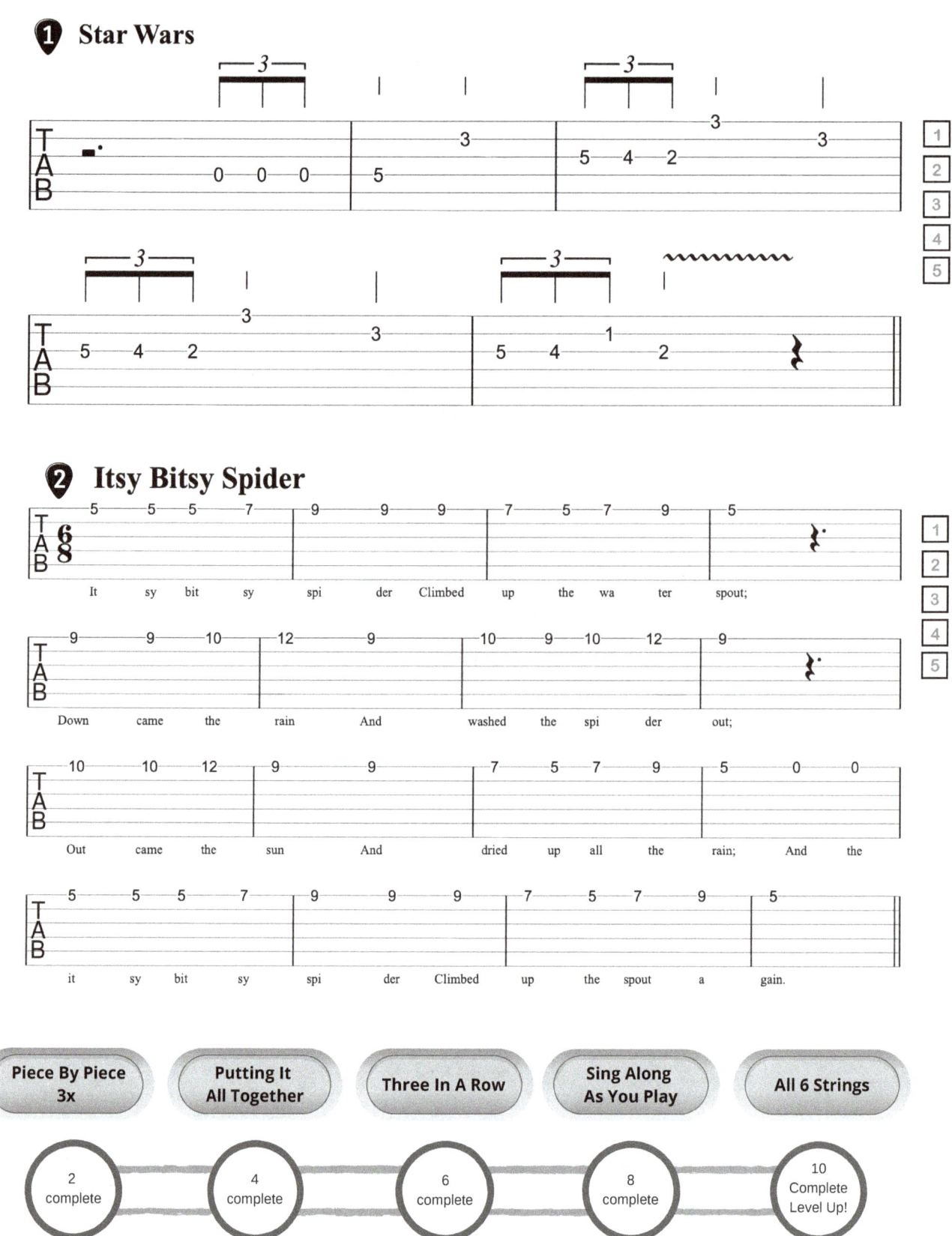

2 Itsy Bitsy Spider

Red Belt Melodies

Here are two classic movie themes from franchises that are forever popular. These examples are long and complex so make sure you learn them slowly.

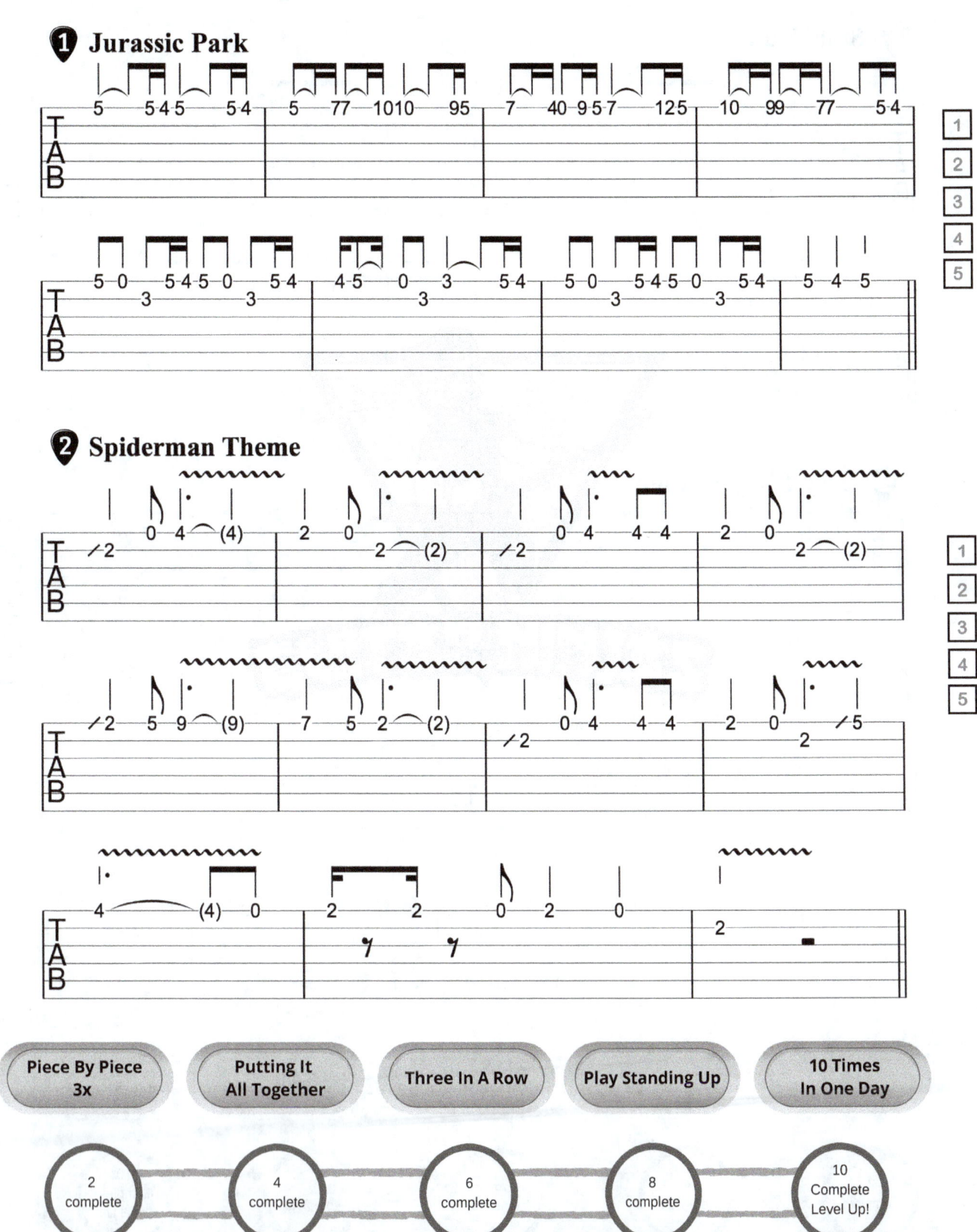

Grey Belt Melodies

We're on the home stretch now and hopefully, these melodies will feel like a breeze! We've mixed up the challenges to keep things fun and exciting!

1 **Minuet in B**

2 **Harry Potter**

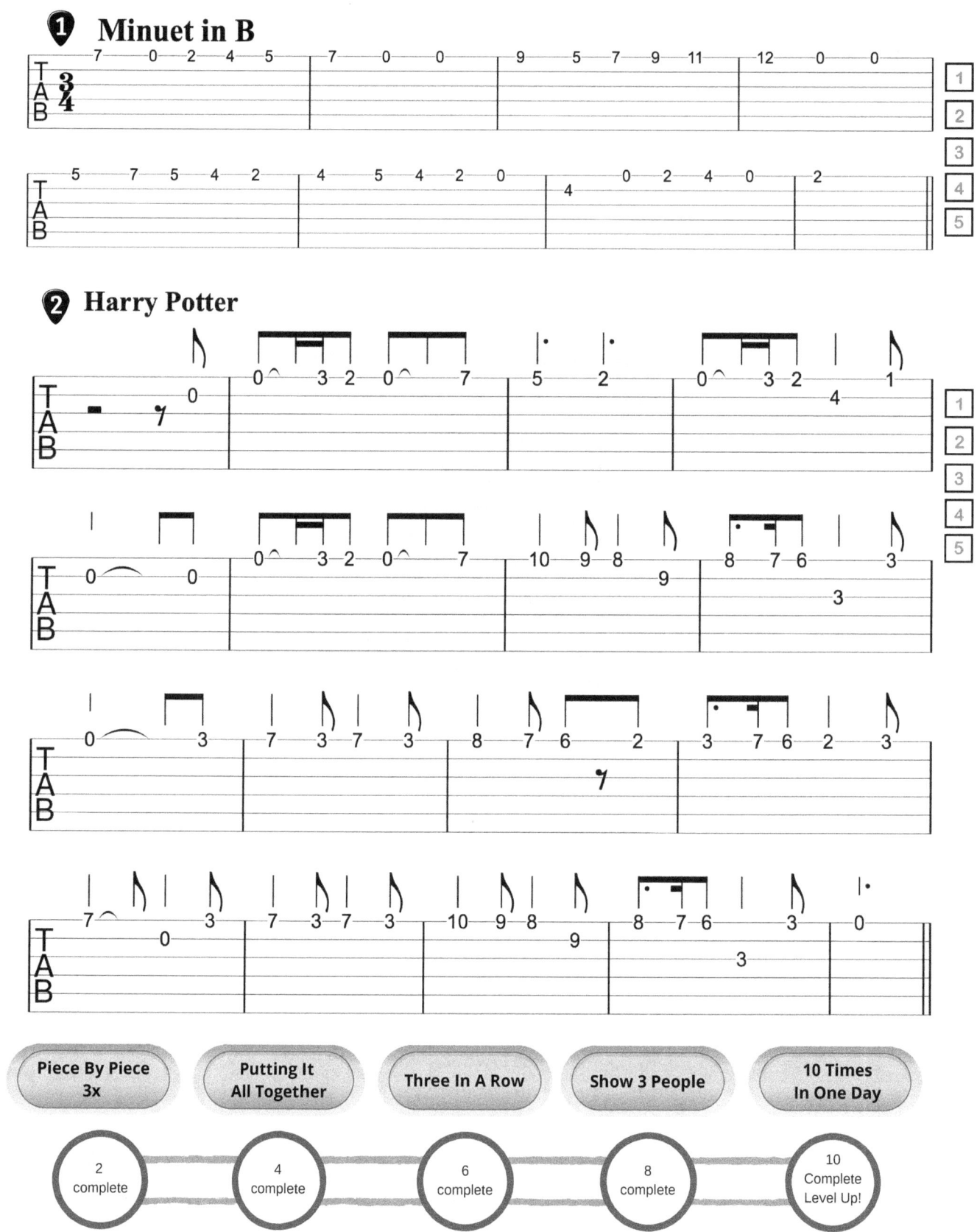

| Piece By Piece 3x | Putting It All Together | Three In A Row | Show 3 People | 10 Times In One Day |

| 2 complete | 4 complete | 6 complete | 8 complete | 10 Complete Level Up! |

Black Belt Melodies

Congratulations on making it to the black belt level! Our last two melodies will definitely be a challenge but you've come this far and there is no turning back! We're certain you'll get these in no time at all!

❶ Happy Birthday

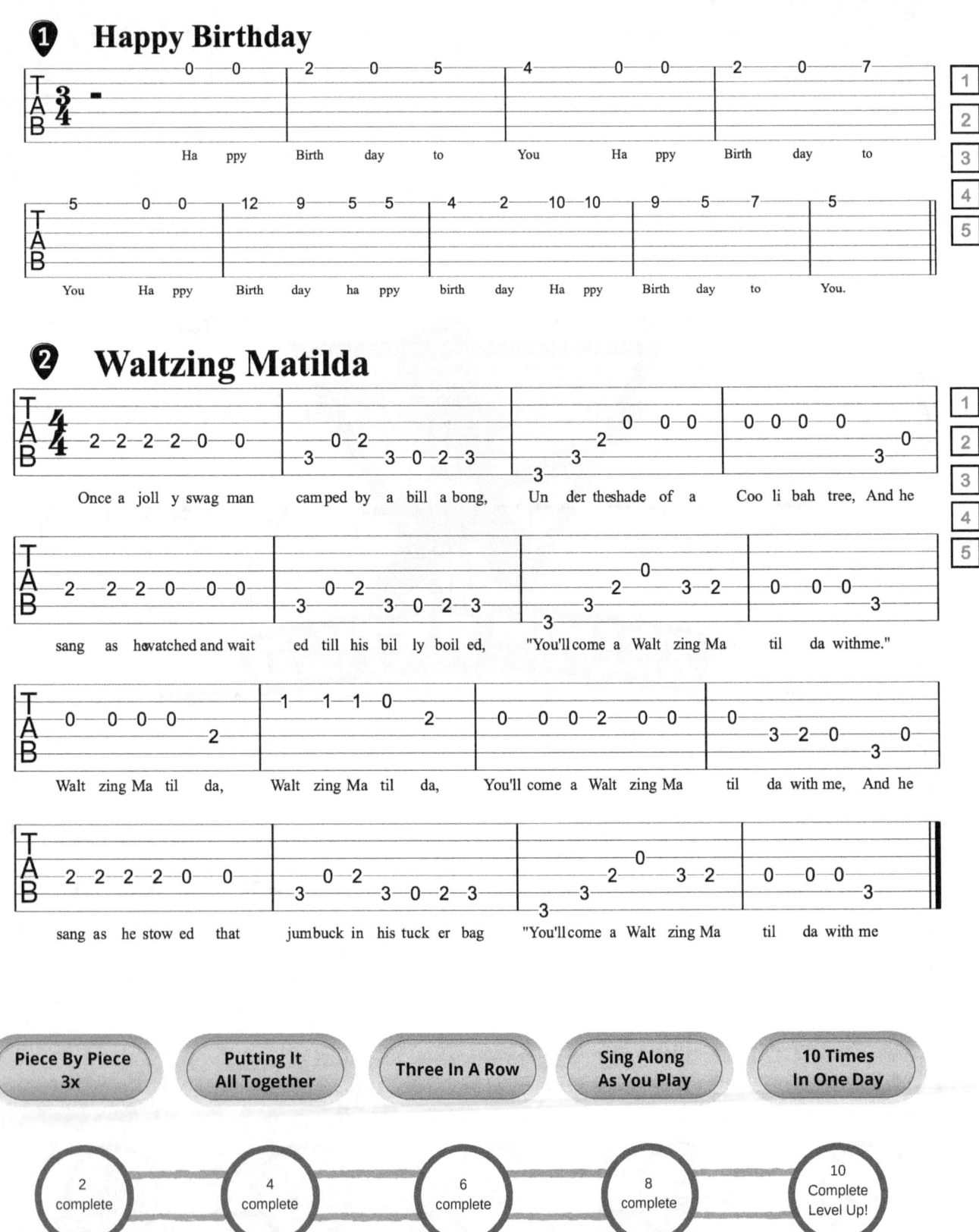

❷ Waltzing Matilda

| Piece By Piece 3x | Putting It All Together | Three In A Row | Sing Along As You Play | 10 Times In One Day |

| 2 complete | 4 complete | 6 complete | 8 complete | 10 Complete Level Up! |

© Guitar Ninjas
Little Ninjas Guitar Method Book
www.GuitarNinjas.com.au

42

Section 4

Riffs

Riffs are short patterns of music that we play on the guitar, and they often repeat over and over.

They're great to learn because they can help improve our timing, sound like the real song relatively quickly and are usually fun and easy to learn.

Riffs are usually played on the lower strings of the guitar and are used as accompaniment parts in songs. By learning different riffs, you'll be able to play them confidently and impress your friends and family with your guitar skills!

So, let's start learning some cool riffs that you can show off to everyone!

White Belt Riffs

A Riff is a short, repeated phrase of music which is usually associated with the most recognisable part of a song.

Riffs are great to learn because they help us improve our timing, and can quickly be learned and played for friends and family.

We'll learn 3 riffs for every level, as well as having some special challenges to help you practice in a variety of fun and enjoyable ways.

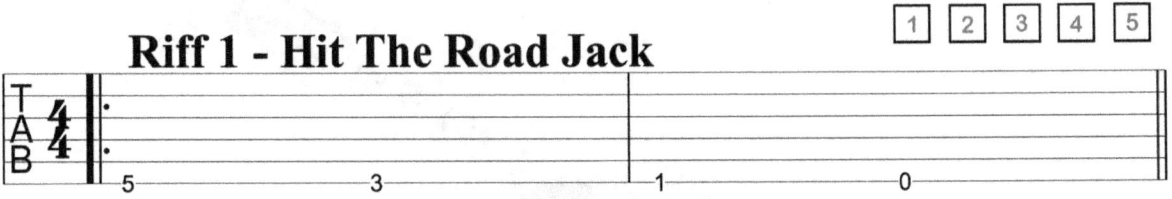

This riff is a great starter because we only needs four notes to play. Don't forget to go through the process of *say it three times, play it three times* when learning riffs.

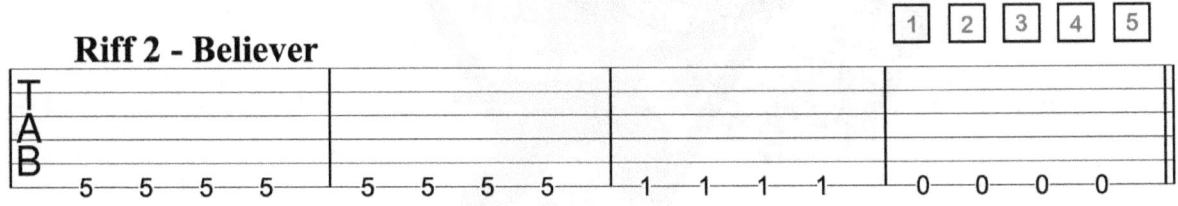

For this riff, we are going to only use 3 notes (fret 5, fret 1 and fret 0) but we are going to pick four times for every bar of music.

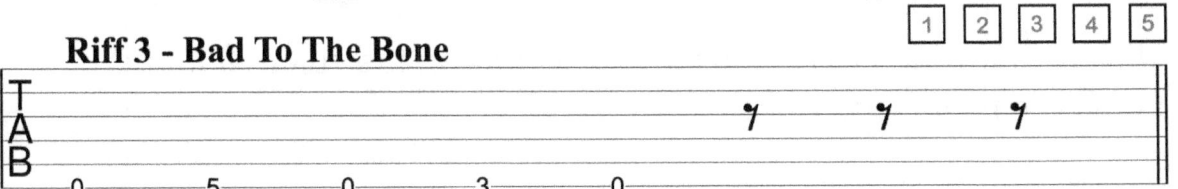

Here is a short 5 note riff. The symbols at the end of the bar are rests that tell you not to play on these counts.

Riff Challenges & Experience Meter

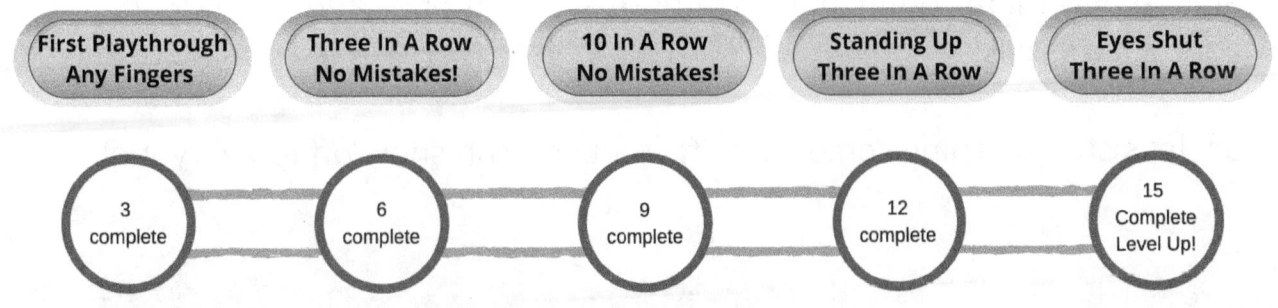

© Guitar Ninjas
Little Ninjas Guitar Method Book
www.GuitarNinjas.com.au

Yellow Belt Riffs

An important element of learning is listening! Make sure you listen to these riffs so you know what they sound like. You could even ask Mum or Dad to help you find these songs online and make a playlist for you.

You have three new riffs to learn, and while you can play them with a single finger, it will be much better to use multiple fingers. Try it out!

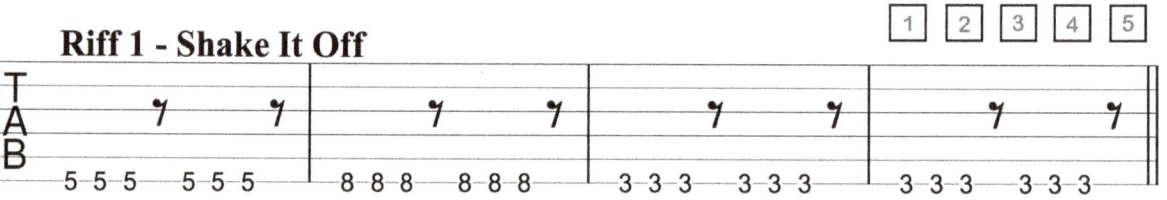

Our first riff is only three notes but we're going to pick six times in each bar. I like to think of it as two groups of three picks per bar.

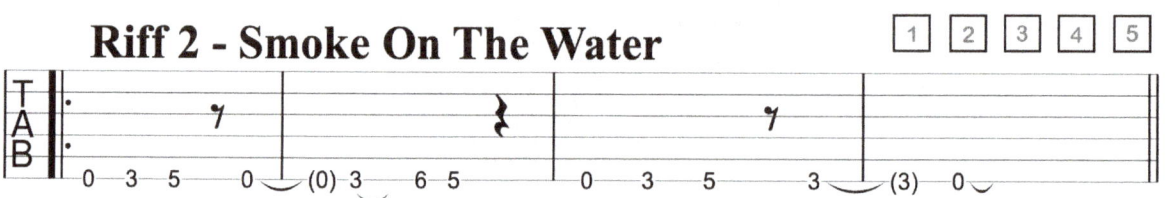

This is probably the greatest riff of all time and will be a great one to show your friends. Your first finger can play fret 3, your third finger can play fret 5 and your pinkie can play 6

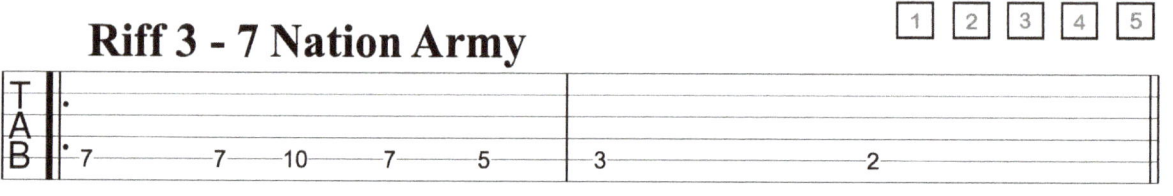

Another popular riff. Use your third finger for fret 10 and your first finger for everything else. Once you learn power chords you can come back and try adding them to your riffs.

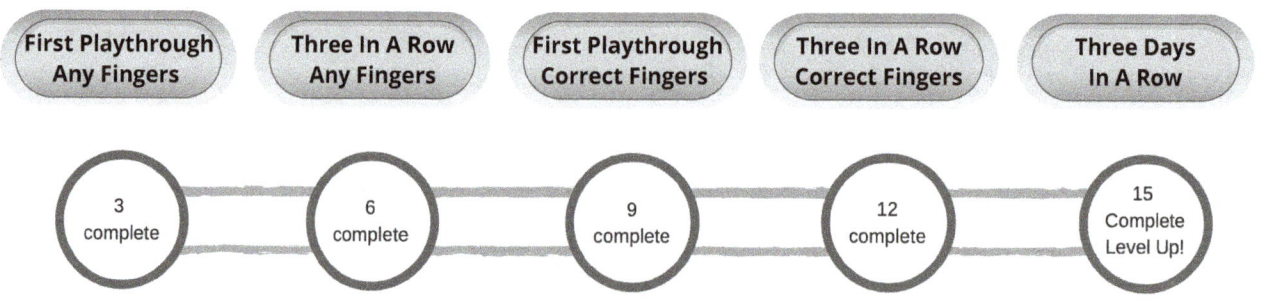

Orange Belt Riffs

All of our riffs have been simplified to single string ideas to make it easier to learn.

Many of the originals were played with power chords. To play a power chord simply add your third finger (or pinkie) two frets higher on the string above the note you are currently playing.

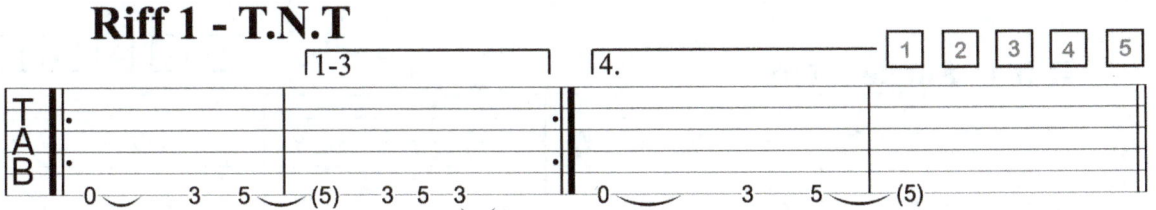

This classic by AC/DC is a must know guitar repertoire track and sounds even better when you play it with power chords!

Another classic riff that sounds good with or without power chords. Make sure you play it on string 5 as written above

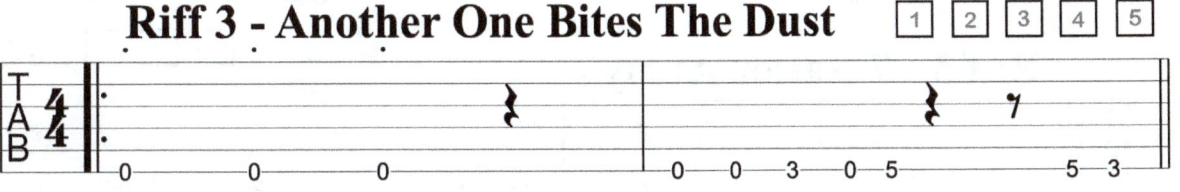

Our last riff for this level is actually played on bass guitar, but we've adapted it here for you to play on your guitar!

Tip: You can learn more about Power Chords on page 57

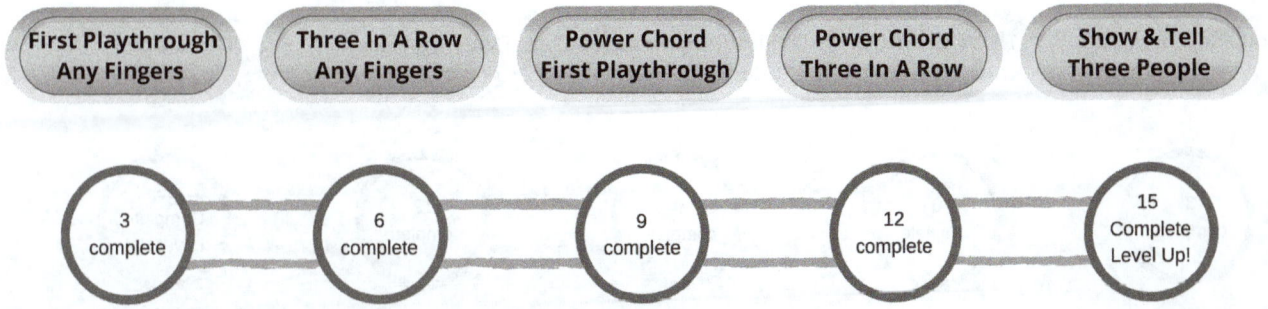

Green Belt Riffs

You should be well and truly in the habit of learning riffs by now so we've changed some of the challenges in order to keep you on your toes.

Don't forget to go back and work on some of your old riffs every now and then. Doing this will keep them fresh in your memory and ready to perform.

Riff 1 - Highway To Hell

Another classic by AC/DC! This is essential guitar repertoire and sounds even better when you play it with power chords!

Riff 2 - Sunshine Of Your Love

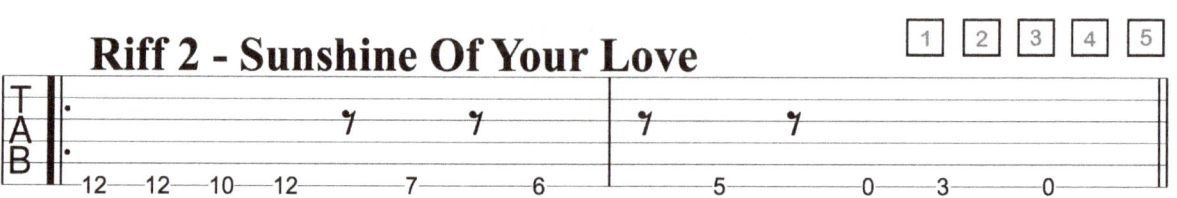

Another classic riff that sounds good with or without powerchords. Don't forget to mute the strings between notes as indicated by the rests.

Riff 3 - When I Come Around

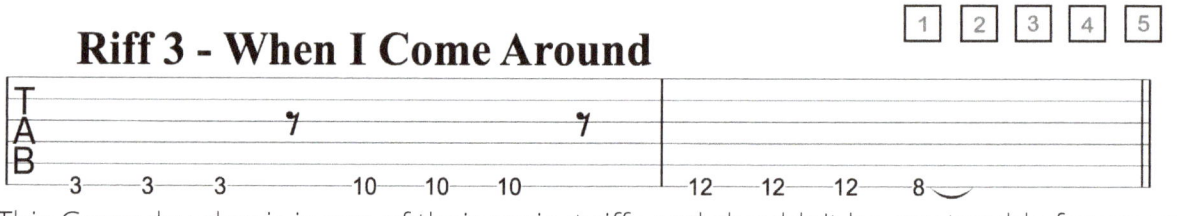

This Greenday classic is one of their easiest riffs and shouldn't be any trouble for you at all! It sounds even better with Power Chords

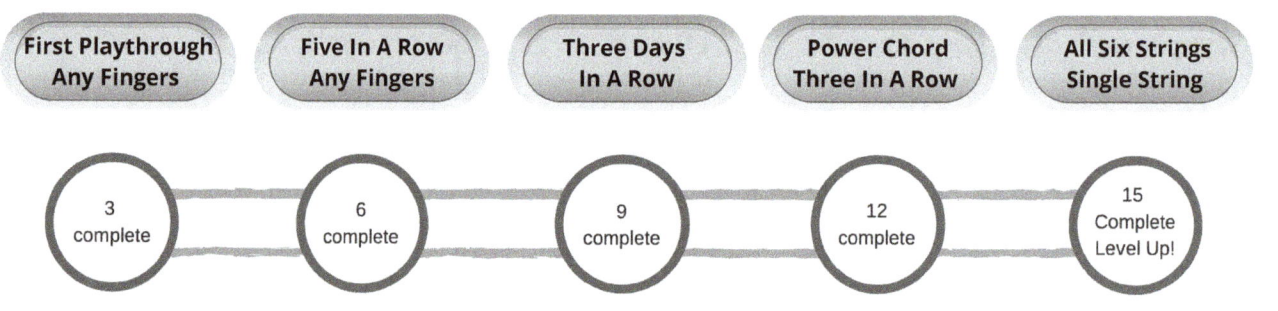

Blue Belt Riffs

We've included even more challenges to keep the riffs fun and interesting. If you don't understand what to do make sure you ask your teacher for help.

If you like a particular challenge from another level you can always try completing it with the new riffs or visa versa, especially if you run out of challenges to complete.

Riff 1 - Iron Man

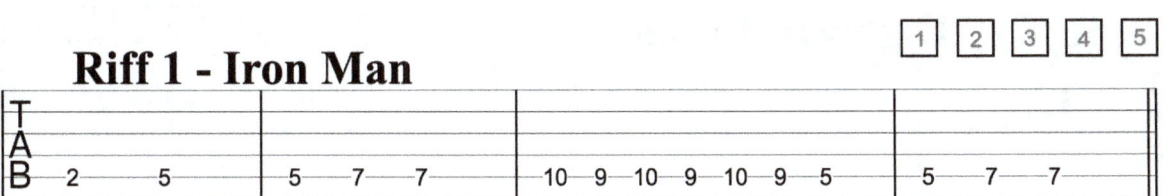

Our first riff entry from the mighty Black Sabbath! - The band that made power chord riffs and heavy metal popular.

Riff 2 - Smells Like Teen Spirit

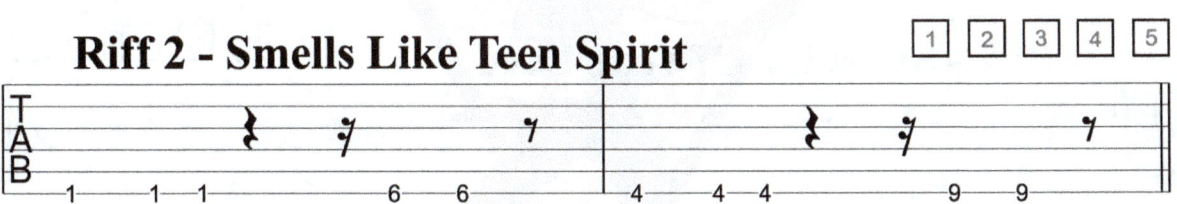

Also making their first appearance is Nirvana, a band known for easy power chord riffs that are great to sing along to.

Riff 3 - Uptown Funk

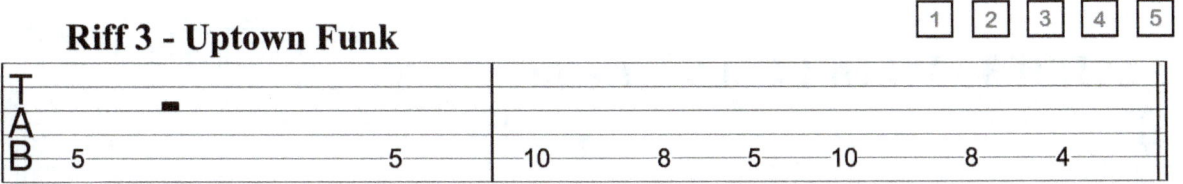

Here is one of the newer riffs in the book, a great funky baseline which we've adapted to the guitar for you!

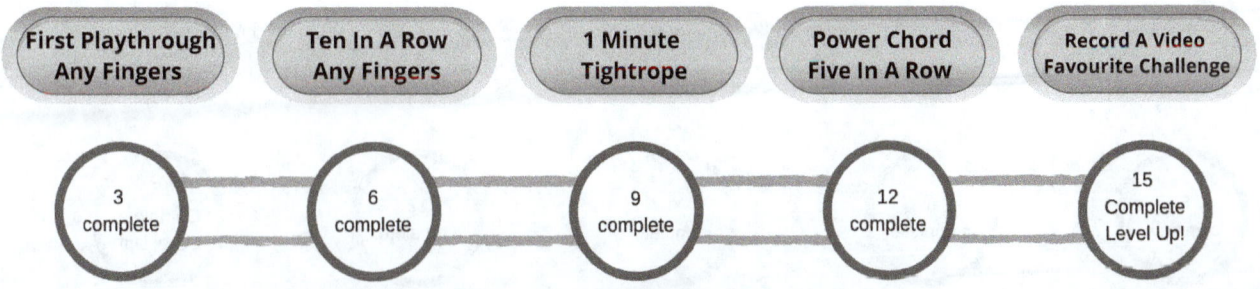

© Guitar Ninjas
Little Ninjas Guitar Method Book
www.GuitarNinjas.com.au

Purple Belt Riffs

We have three more riffs and some more unique challenges for you at the purple belt level.

If you haven't gone back to play over your white, yellow or orange riffs in a while (or ever) you should go back and hopefully see how easy they are now that you're playing at a purple belt level.

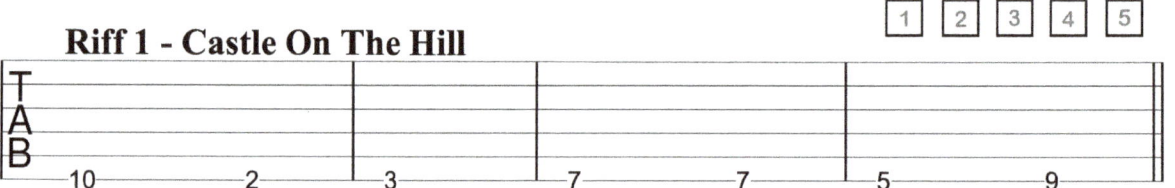

Here is a great riff played on string 6. The last note leads back into the first note on every repeat of the riff!

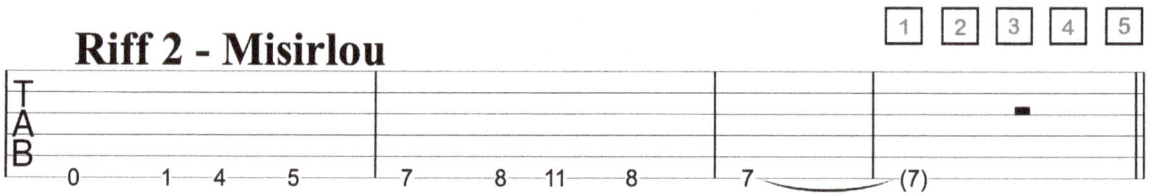

This song is over 1000 years old and is adapted from an old greek folk tune. Dick Dale revamped it and made it famous in the 50's as a surf rock tune!

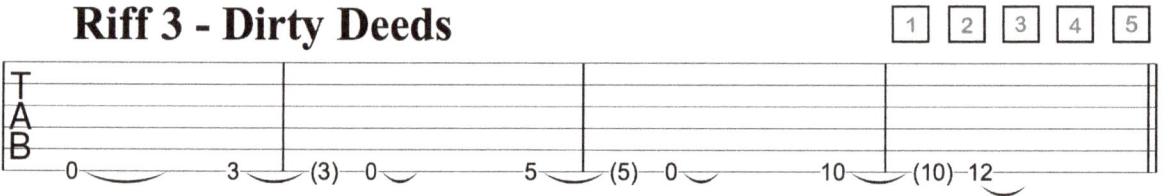

This riff sounds equally great played on open strings and using power chords. Hopefully mum and dad are helping you find and listen to the songs online so you can hear how they sound.

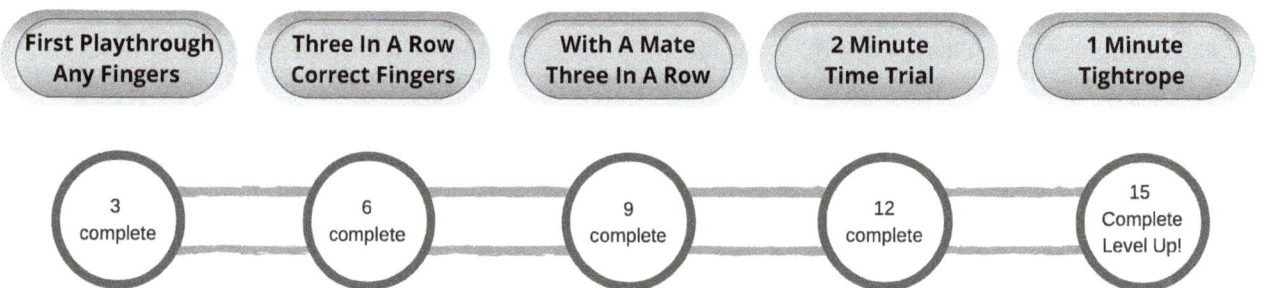

Red Belt Riffs

Here are some great tunes which have been featured in movies and TV shows. Best of all is that they can be played as riffs on the guitar!

Riff 1 - Peter Gunn Theme

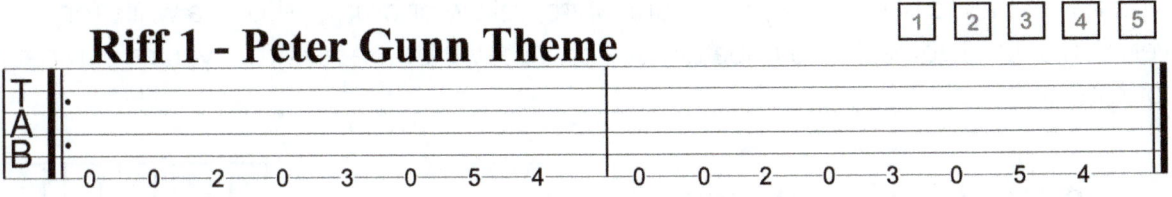

This is one of the greatest themes from one of the greatest movies of all time. It repeats the same 8-note pattern over & over. Use a different finger for each note.

Riff 2 - Batman

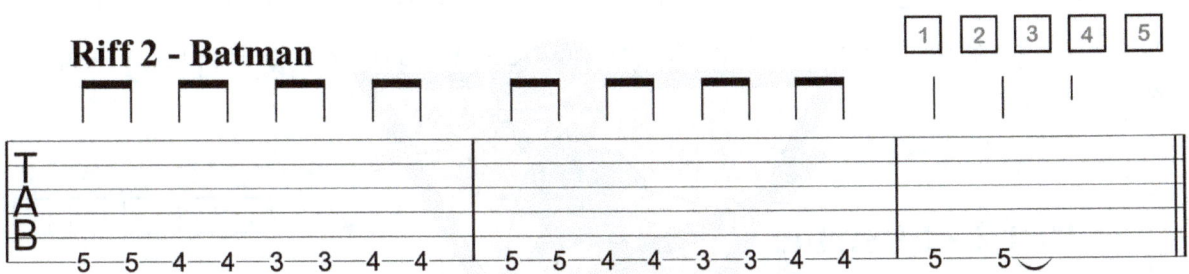

Here is a popular riff from the original Batman TV show. Try moving it around a 12 bar blues pattern.

Riff 3 - I Like To Move It Move It

Here is a popular riff that came back to prominence in the Madagascar movies. Once you get the basics down try to play it across two strings using multiple fingers.

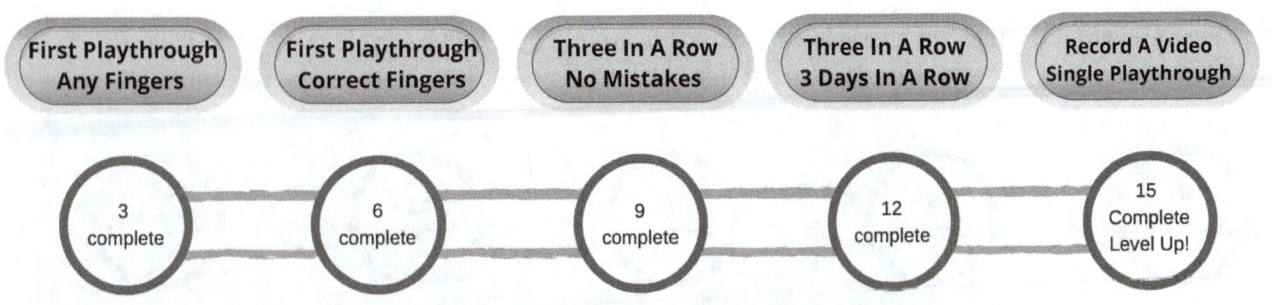

Grey Belt Riffs

For the Grey Belt level we're going to go back to some classic rock and heavy metal riffs.

All of these riffs are played across multiple strings and will challenge you to coordinate your fingers to the right frets.

Riff 1 - Crazy Train

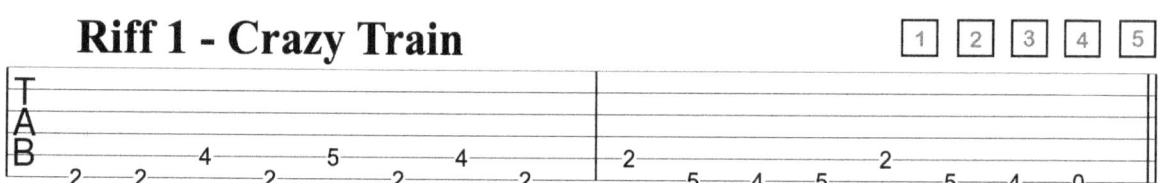

This is one of the greatest heavy metal riffs of all time and is sure to impress your friends.

Riff 2 - Rock You Like A Hurricane

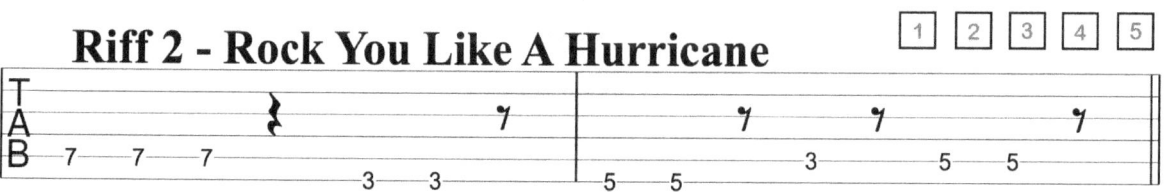

Another classic riff that sounds good with or without powerchords. Don't forget to mute the strings between notes.

Riff 3 - Breaking The Law

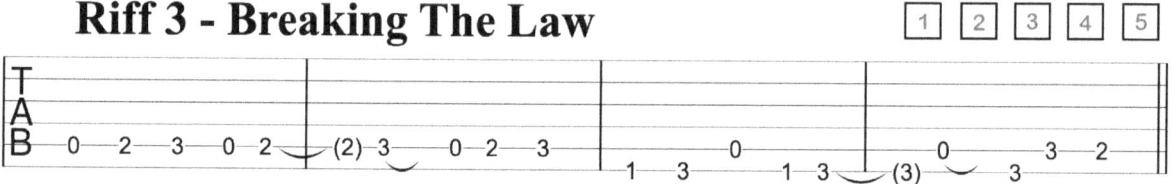

This riff combines multiple fingers, multiple strings and open notes into one tricky challenge for you to play.

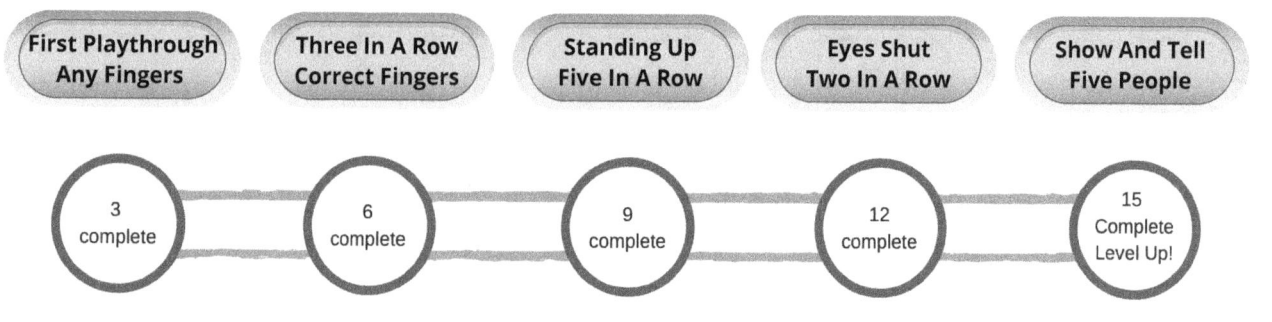

Black Belt Riffs

Congratulations on making it to the end of the riff section for this book. We're going to challenge you with some final riffs, two of which are played across three or more strings.

Happy Riffing!

Riff 1 - Back In Black

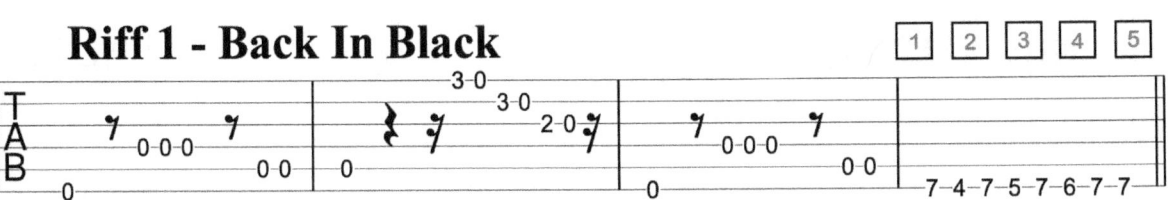

This is another one of the greatest rock riffs of all time! You can even play the first and third bars using open string power chords.

Riff 2 - Beat It

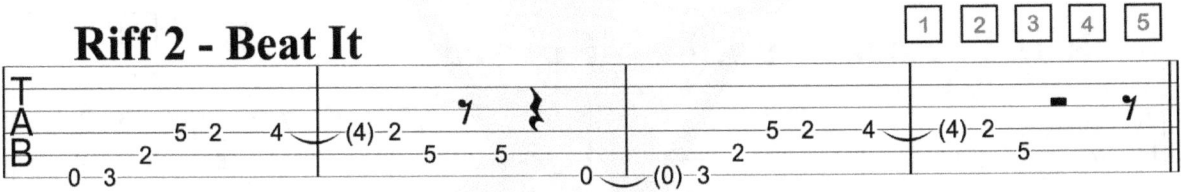

Here is another classic riff that will challenge you to use all four of your fingers. You won't need to use power chords at all for this one.

Riff 3 - Hold The Line

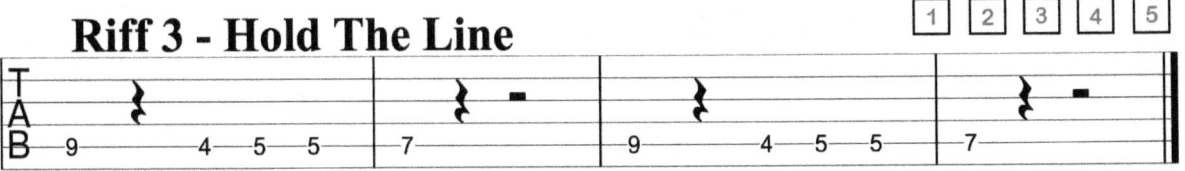

We're actually finishing on an easy riff as a reward for all your hard work so far. Make sure you work your way up to power chords and then include a powerslide between the first and second notes!

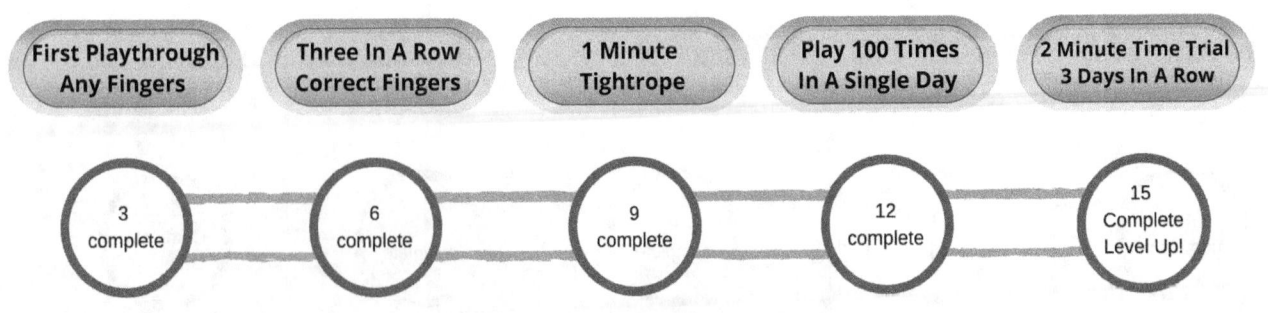

Section 5

Chords & Progressions

Chords are a very important part of playing the guitar and are often what we think of first when it comes to playing songs around the campfire.

The problem with this is that most of these chord shapes are simply too difficult for little fingers to play.

It's also quite a lot for our younger learners to process and try to remember.

As a result, we're simplifying the process and using three levels to play our chords and progressions.

The Level Up System For Chords

We will be simplifying chords and progressions into three levels for our fretting hand and three levels for our picking hand.

Fretting Hand Level 1 involves playing along to progressions using one finger on one string. This is known as playing a bass line and is often what a bass player will do within a band context.

Fretting Hand Level 2 involves turning our bass line into Power Chords which are a simplified movable chord shape containing only two notes by adding an extra finger to what we've already learned.

Fretting Hand Level 3 involves learning two additional movable chord shapes (one for major chords and one for minor chords) which we can play using just one finger. This makes playing chords easier both physically and mentally as we only need to memorise two shapes and practice moving them around instead of dozens of shapes.

Picking Hand Level 1 involves picking or strumming just one note and letting it ring out for four counts (or 6 notes in 6/8 time).

Picking Hand Level 2 involves picking or strumming our notes or chord once per beat. This usually equates to four picks per bar of music but will sometimes involve 3 times or 6 times when playing with odd time signatures like 3/4 or 6/8

Picking Hand Level 3 involves picking or strumming a simplified rhythm. It could be two strums per beat or a simple rhythm pattern like Down, Down-Up Down, Down. Your teacher will assign this in your lesson.

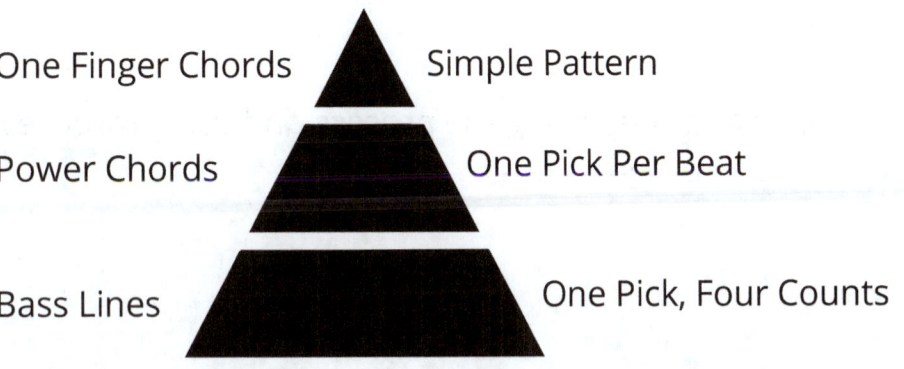

© Guitar Ninjas
Little Ninjas Guitar Method Book
www.GuitarNinjas.com.au

Level 1 - How To Play Basslines

In order to play along to any song you just need to play the note on String 6 that matches the letter of the chord being played.

For example, If the chord progression is G, D, Em & C then we just need to play the notes G, D, E & C on string 6.

Use the fretboard diagram of string 6 below to figure out which frets to play:

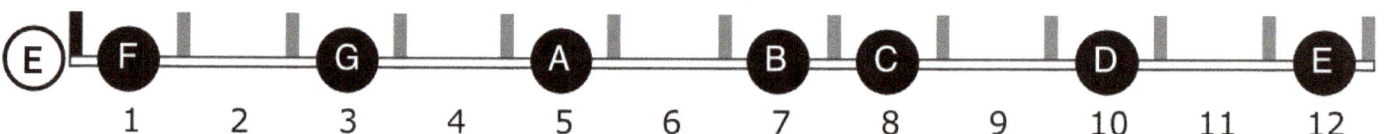

Hopefully, you came up with these answers:

G = Fret 3   D = Fret 10   E = Fret 0 or 12*   C = Fret 8

So in order to play along to this chord progression (or any song that uses it) you only need to play frets 3, 10, 12 or 8 in time with the music.

Let's see how this would look as Guitar Music.

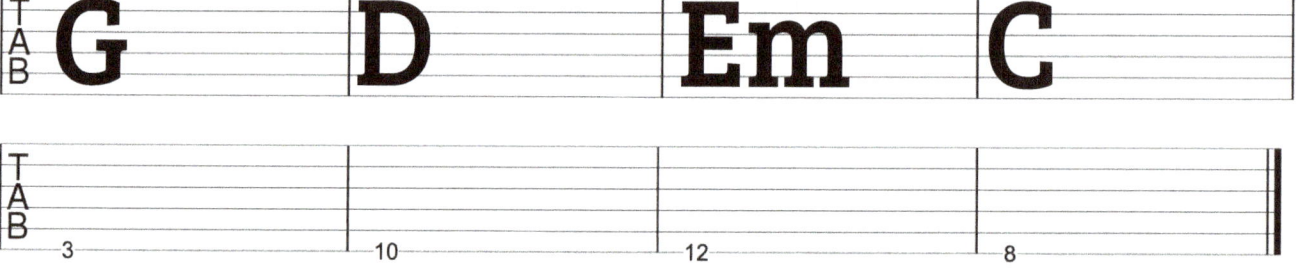

How to play along to this chord progression:

- Start by playing fret 3 and letting it ring out for four counts.
- then play fret 10 and let it ring our for four counts
- then play fret 12 and let it ring our for four counts
- lastly, play fret 8 and let it ring our for four counts before going back to 3 and starting over.

Of course, this is going to sound simple, but that's the point. Once you get the hang of it you can add more notes and to make it more challenging, and more interesting.

*E is found at both 0 and fret 12 on string 6. It's your choice which one you play

Level 1 Chord Progressions

A **Chord Progression** is when we have two or more chords and play them one after the other. Most of your favourite songs are just chord progressions with singing over the top.

For Level 1 you will be presented with 5 chord progressions. Your job is to figure out how to play them as basslines on string 6.

First convert each chord to a number on string 6, then play it on your guitar.

Fret Numbers: G = ____ Em = ____ C = ____ D = ____ | 1 | 2 | 3 | 4 | 5 |

❶ G / / / | Em / / / | C / / / | D / / /

Fret Numbers: A = ____ D = ____ E = ____ D = ____ | 1 | 2 | 3 | 4 | 5 |

❷ A / / / | D / / / | E / / / | D / / /

Fret Numbers: C = ____ G = ____ Am = ____ F = ____ | 1 | 2 | 3 | 4 | 5 |

❸ C / / / | G / / / | Am / / / | F / / /

Fret Numbers: C = ____ F = ____ Dm = ____ G = ____ | 1 | 2 | 3 | 4 | 5 |

❹ C / / / | F / / / | Dm / / / | G / / /

Fret Numbers: Bm = ____ A = ____ G = ____ D = ____ | 1 | 2 | 3 | 4 | 5 |

❺ Bm / / / | A / / / | G / / / | D / / /

Chord Progression Challenges & Experience Meter

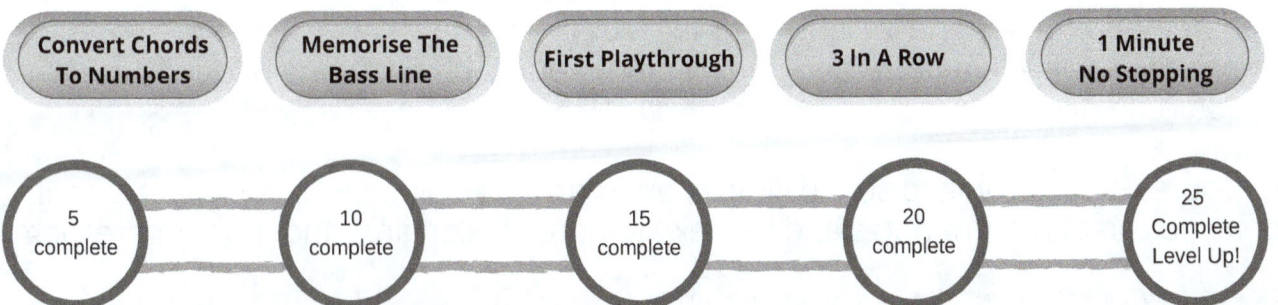

Convert Chords To Numbers | Memorise The Bass Line | First Playthrough | 3 In A Row | 1 Minute No Stopping

5 complete — 10 complete — 15 complete — 20 complete — 25 Complete Level Up!

Level 2 - How To Play Power Chords

A **Chord** is made by playing three or more notes on the guitar at the same time using a strum. On guitar, we have special chords called **Power Chords** which we can play using only two notes!

Power Chords get their name because they sound big and powerful, and are used in loud, high-energy music like rock, metal, punk and grunge. Power Chords are great for beginners because they are all played using one shape, which we can move to any fret on the 6th or 5th string using only two fingers.

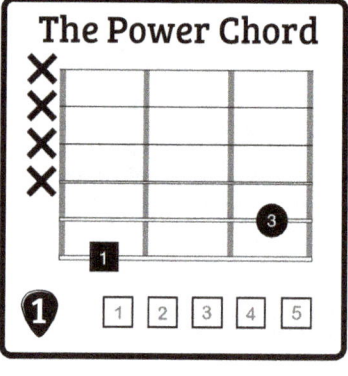

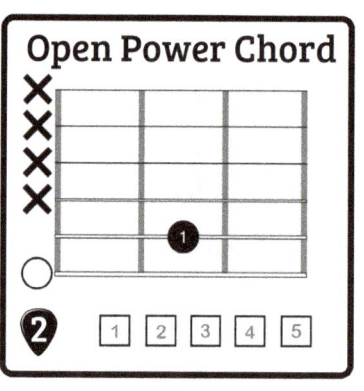

To play a Power Chord you need to put your first finger on any chosen fret on string 6, and then put your third finger two frets higher on string 5.

For example, if you put your first finger on String 6 Fret 5, your third finger will go on String 5 Fret 7. This would be called an A Power Chord (written as A5) because it starts on an A note at the 5th fret of String 6. Let's take a look at some power chords below.

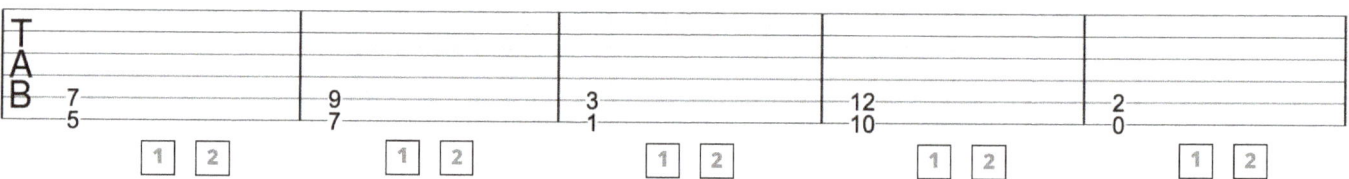

Naming Power Chords

Power Chords take on the name of the note on which they are played from. This note is called the **Root Note**.
So if you want to play a G Power Chord, you find the G note on string 6 (fret three) and build the power chord shape on top of it. Below is a diagram of the notes on string 6 to help you find where to play each chord.

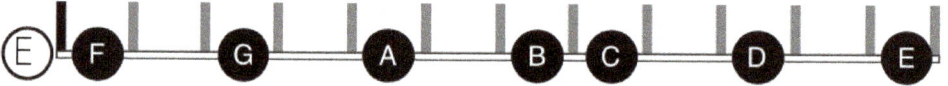

Open String Power Chords: When the note you are trying to play is the open string use your first finger to play the 2nd fret of string 5.

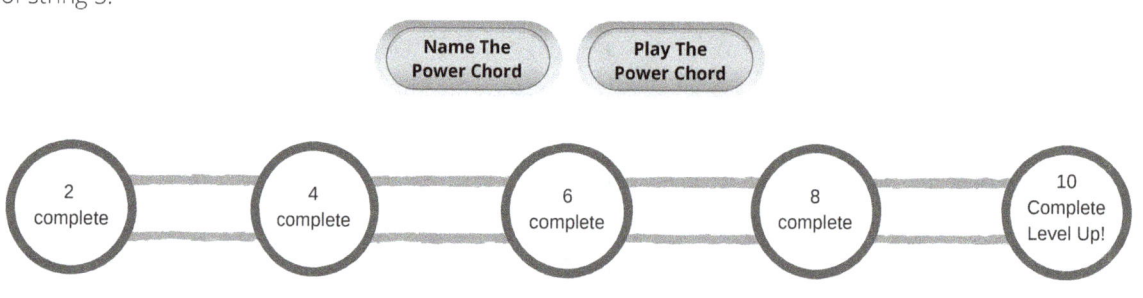

© Guitar Ninjas
Little Ninjas Guitar Method Book
www.GuitarNinjas.com.au

Level 2 Chord Progressions

Play the following chord progressions using Power Chords.

Start by converting the progression into the fret numbers on string 6.

Then practice playing them until you can change between all the chords smoothly.

Fret Numbers: F = ____ G = ____ Am = ____ C = ____   1 2 3 4 5

1 | F / / / | G / / / | Am / / / | C / / / |

Fret Numbers: A = ____ D = ____ E = ____ G = ____   1 2 3 4 5

2 | A / / / | D / / / | E / / / | G / / / |

Fret Numbers: C = ____ G = ____ Am = ____ F = ____   1 2 3 4 5

3 | C / / / | G / / / | Am / / / | F / / / |

Fret Numbers: G = ____ D = ____ Em = ____ C = ____   1 2 3 4 5

4 | G / / / | D / / / | Em / / / | C / / / |

Fret Numbers: D = ____ G = ____ A = ____ Bm = ____   1 2 3 4 5

5 | D / / / | G / / / | A / / / | Bm / / / |

Chord Progression Challenges & Experience Meter

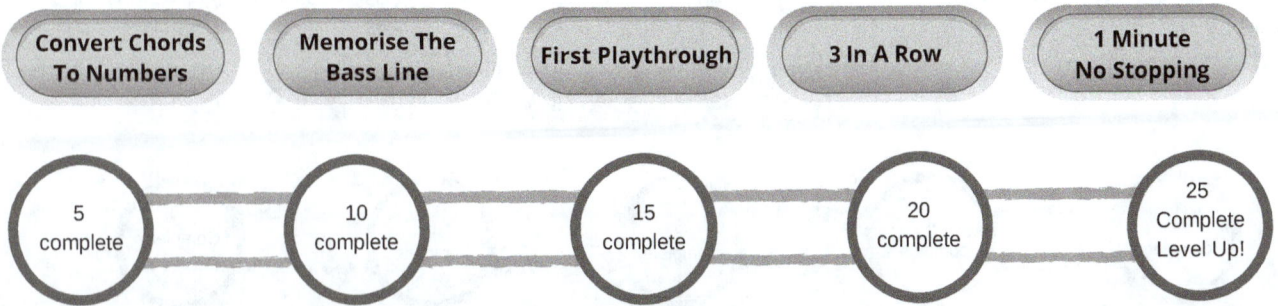

| Convert Chords To Numbers | Memorise The Bass Line | First Playthrough | 3 In A Row | 1 Minute No Stopping |

| 5 complete | 10 complete | 15 complete | 20 complete | 25 Complete Level Up! |

Level 3 - How To Play One Finger Triads

Level 3 in our Level-Up system introduces Triads: the smallest form of a chord that contains just three notes!

We are going to learn two new chord shapes, a Minor Triad shape and a Major Triad shape both of which allow us to play major and minor chords with just one finger!

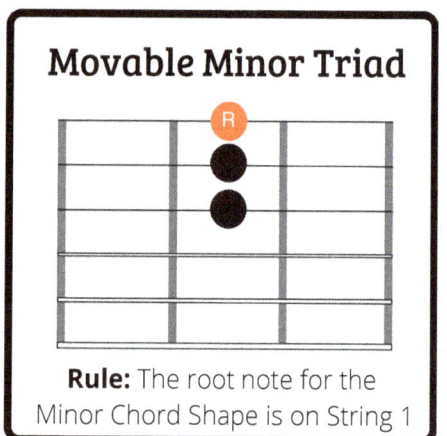

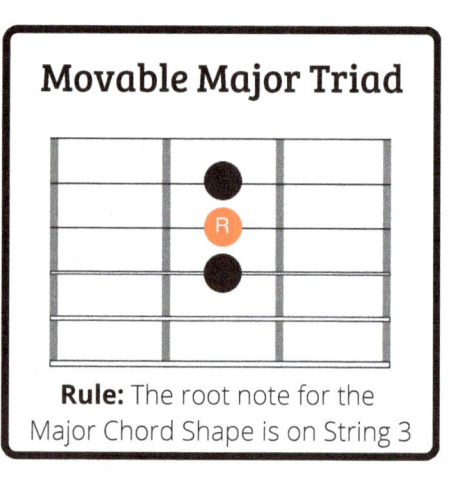

You can play any Minor Chord using the Movable Minor Triad Shape on the first three strings. Simply align your finger with the root note on String 1, bar it across the first three strings and strum. EG. If you want to play a G Minor Chord then play the shape at fret 3.

The Major chord works the exact same way except that you will use the shape on strings 2-4 instead. Line your finger up with the root note on string 3 and strum. Eg. If you want to play a D chord you will play the shape at fret 7 but strum strings 2, 3 & 4. The notes along strings 1 and 3 are given below as a reference. (note that the open position works too).

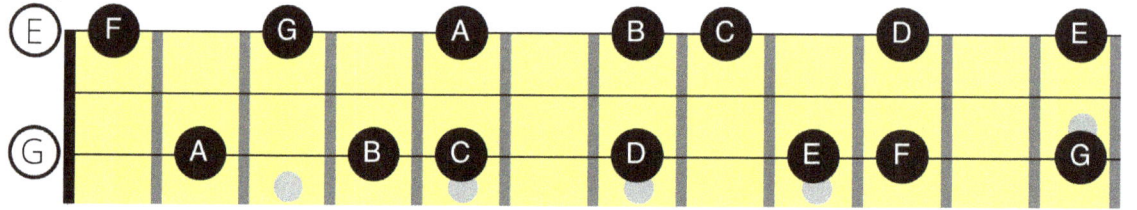

Try playing these chords using the new Movable One Finger Triad Shapes above

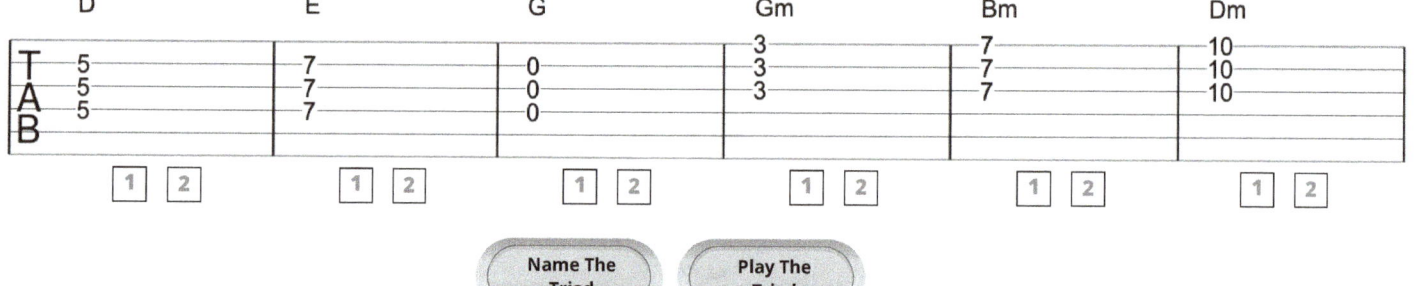

Level 3 Chord Progressions

Play the following chord progressions using One Finger Chords.

Start by converting the progression into the fret numbers using string 3 for Major Chords and string 1 for Minor Chords.

Then practice playing them until you can change between all the chords smoothly.

Fret Numbers: C = ____   F = ____   G = ____   [1] [2] [3] [4] [5]

1   C / / /   F / / /   G / / /   F / / /

Fret Numbers: Cm = ____   Dm = ____   Gm = ____   [1] [2] [3] [4] [5]

2   Cm / / /   Dm / / /   Gm / / /   Cm / / /

Fret Numbers: A = ____   D = ____   Bm = ____   G = ____   [1] [2] [3] [4] [5]

3   A / / /   D / / /   Bm / / /   G / / /

Fret Numbers: Am = ____   Dm = ____   E = ____   G = ____   [1] [2] [3] [4] [5]

4   Am / / /   Dm / / /   E / / /   G / / /

Fret Numbers: C = ____   G = ____   Em = ____   F = ____   [1] [2] [3] [4] [5]

5   C / / /   G / / /   Em / / /   F / / /

Chord Progression Challenges

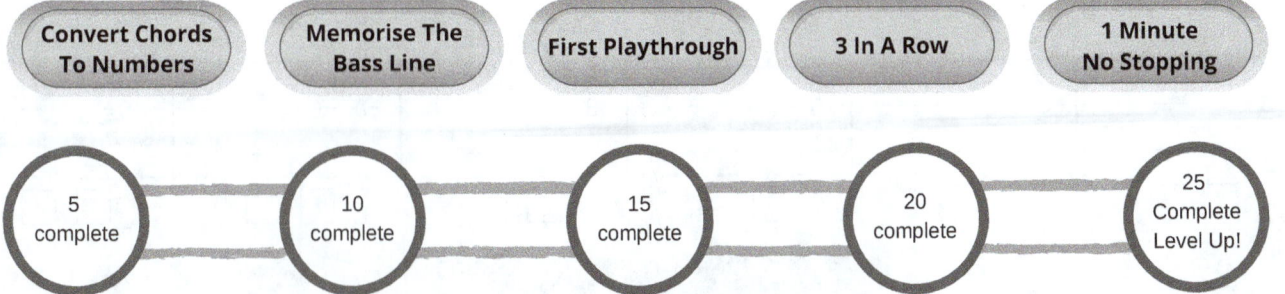

Convert Chords To Numbers	Memorise The Bass Line	First Playthrough	3 In A Row	1 Minute No Stopping

5 complete	10 complete	15 complete	20 complete	25 Complete Level Up!

Section 6

Reading & Rhythms

Learning how to read music is an important skill for all aspiring guitar players.

But don't worry, we'll keep it simple by focusing on how to read Guitar Tab. Guitar Tab is a special kind of notation that makes it easy to start playing along on the guitar right away!

We'll also learn the names of the notes and their rhythms, so we can understand how long to play each note and keep a strong sense of timing while playing music.

With these skills, you'll be able to read music and play your favourite songs on the guitar with confidence! Let's get started!

Little Ninjas Note Reading 1

The guitar is one of the easiest instruments to learn because we can use numbers to tell us where to put our fingers instead of learning how to read standard musical notation.

When it comes to reading Guitar Music you need to remember two things:

- The number is the fret you need to put your finger on.
- The line the number is on is the string you need to be playing on.

Use the examples below to help you practice reading Guitar Tabs by first reading and saying the fret numbers aloud, before trying to play it on your guitar. S = Say it, P = Play It

Notes On String 1

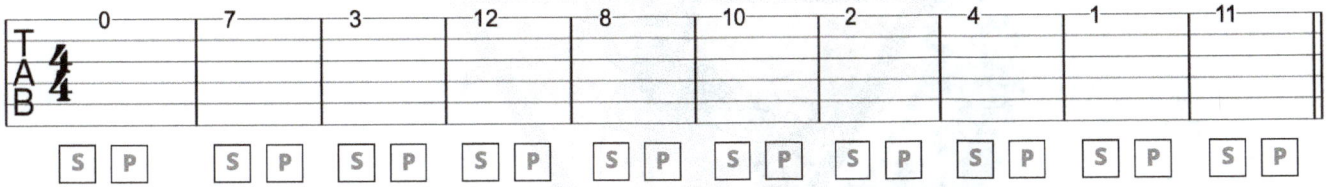

Notes On String 2

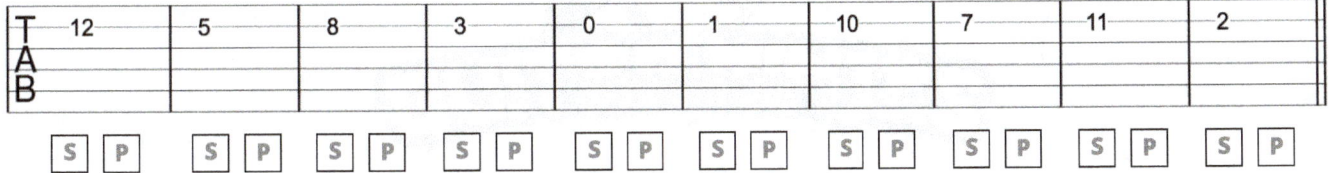

Notes On String 3

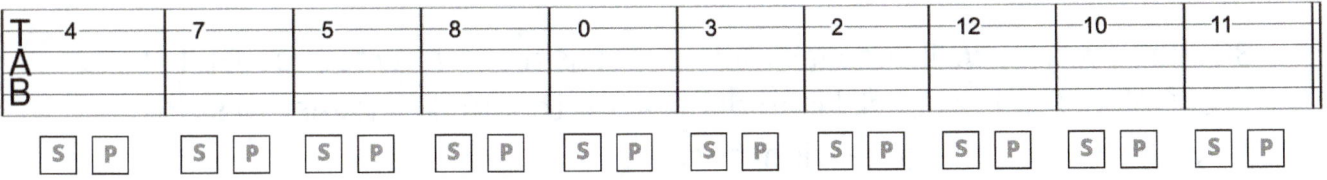

Reading Challenges & Experience Meter

Say It   **Play It**

| 10 complete | 20 complete | 30 complete | 45 complete | 60 Complete Level Up! |

© Guitar Ninjas
Little Ninjas Guitar Method Book
www.GuitarNinjas.com.au

Little Ninjas Note Reading 2

We're going to continue learning how to read guitar music with some examples on the thicker strings.

Remember, when it comes to reading Guitar Music you need to remember two things:

- The number is the fret you need to put your finger on.
- The line the number is on is the string you need to be playing on.

Use the examples below to help you practice reading Guitar Tabs by first reading and saying the fret numbers aloud, before trying to play it on your guitar. S = Say it, P = Play It

Notes On String 4

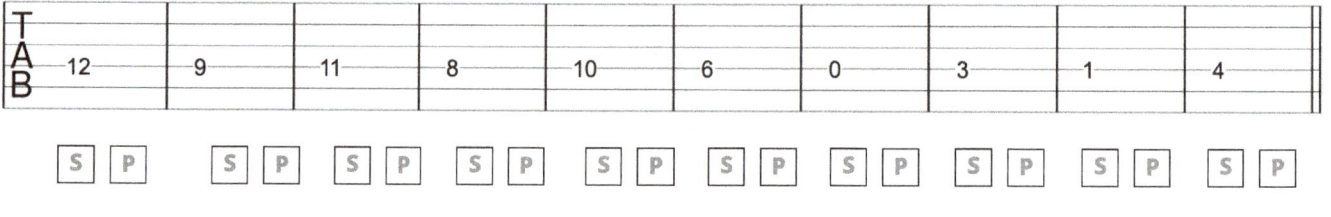

Notes On String 5

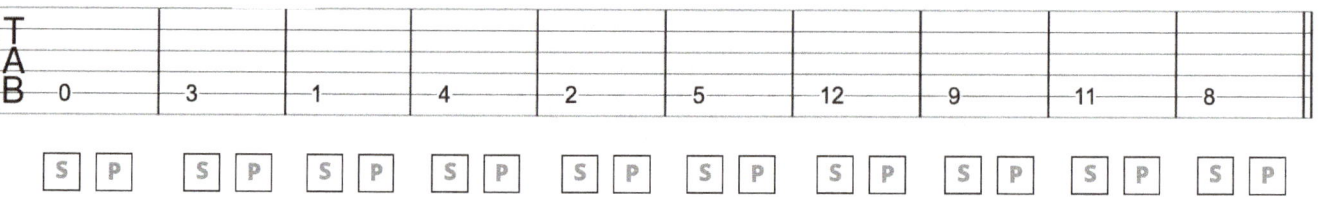
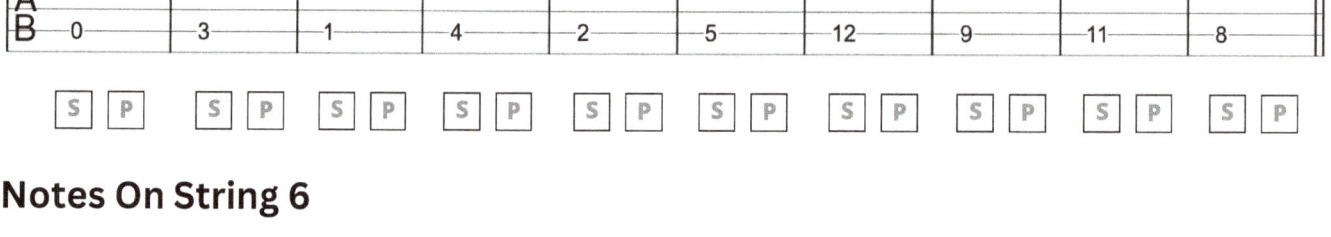

Notes On String 6

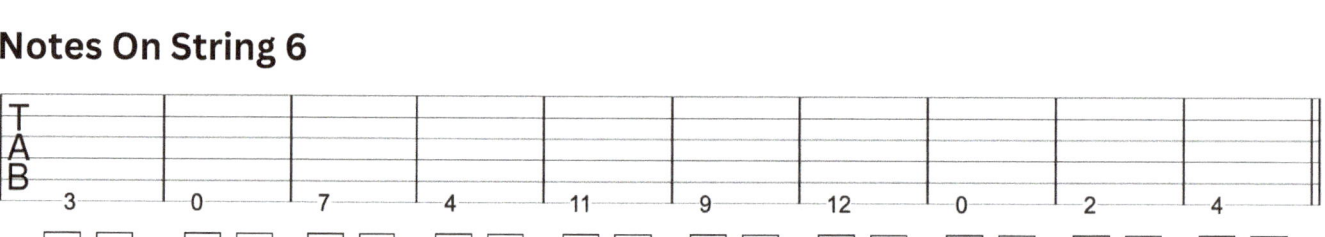

Reading Challenges & Experience Meter

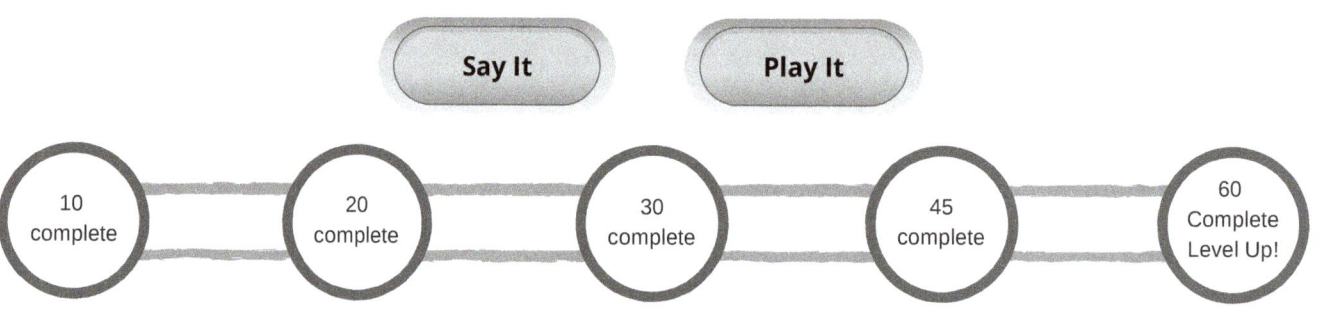

© Guitar Ninjas
Little Ninjas Guitar Method Book
www.GuitarNinjas.com.au

Little Ninjas Note Reading 3

Now that you're getting better at reading guitar music we're going to challenge you to read across multiple strings!

Remember, when it comes to reading Guitar Music you need to remember two things:

- The number is the fret you need to put your finger on.
- The line the number is on is the string you need to be playing on.

Use the examples below to help you practice reading Guitar Tabs by first reading and saying the fret numbers aloud, before trying to play it on your guitar. S = Say it, P = Play It

Notes On Strings 1-3

```
T  0                  12              9              7          11          5
A        1                  3               8              11         12         8
B
```

S P   S P   S P   S P   S P   S P   S P   S P   S P

Notes On String 4-6

```
T                   7              10                           4
A        3               9                      11                  1
B  6                                12                   3
```

S P   S P   S P   S P   S P   S P   S P   S P   S P

Notes On All Six Strings

```
T                               1         12
A              7         8                     10              6
B  0     5                                           4
                                          3
```

S P   S P   S P   S P   S P   S P   S P   S P   S P

Reading Challenges & Experience Meter

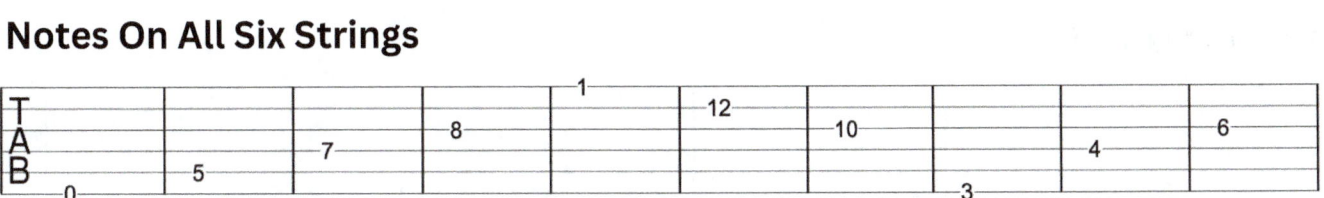

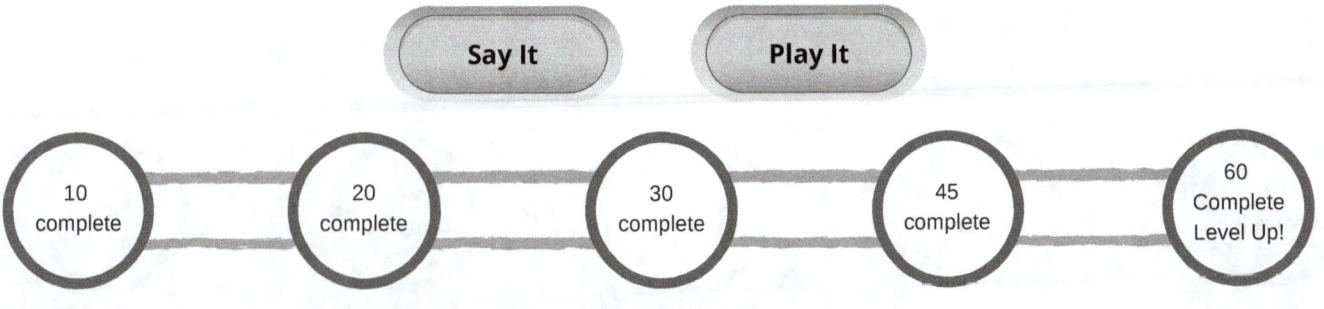

White Belt Rhythm

Musical Notes come in a variety of shapes. The shape of a note tells us its **Rhythm** value, which is a fancy way of saying how many counts it goes for.

Each note shape has both an American name and an English name, We can also match each note to a set of syllables called **Rhythm Syllables** which will help us learn the rhythms and feel the timing more easily.

Being able to read notes and know their timing value is essential to developing good timing and is the first step in our journey of reading music notation.

The Whole Note

4 Counts

English Name: Semibreve
Rhythm Name: Ta-2-3-4

The Half Note

2 Counts

English Name: Minim
Rhythm Name: To-oo

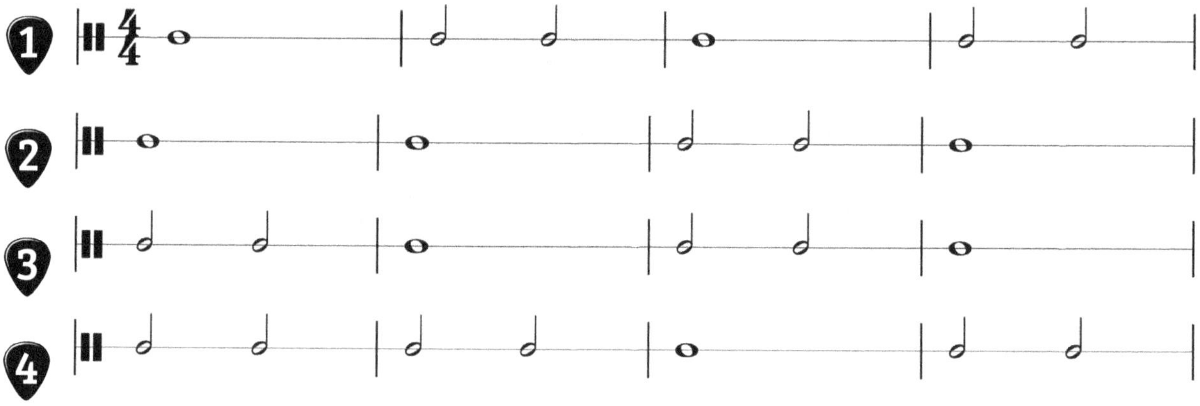

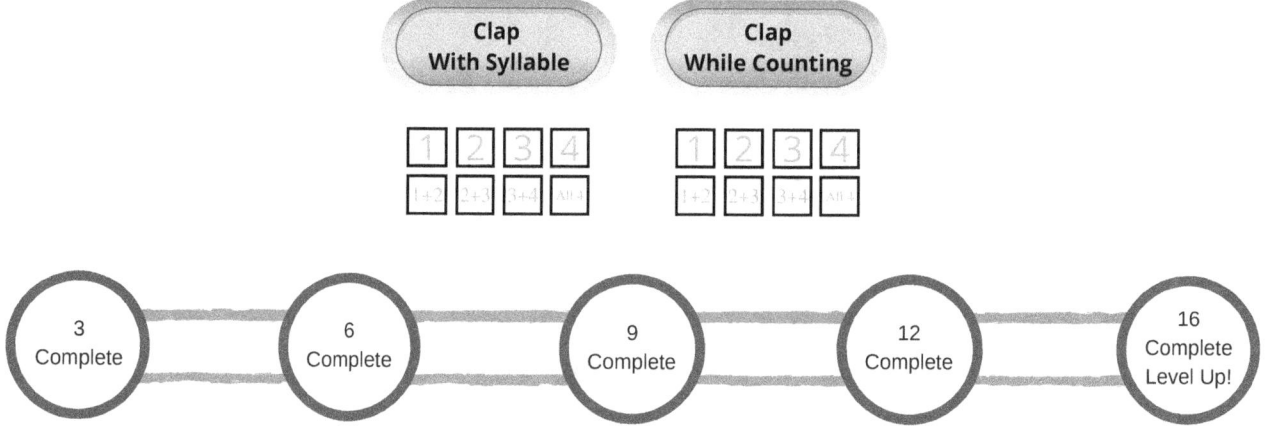

Rhythm Challenges & Experience Meter

Clap
With Syllable

Clap
While Counting

© Guitar Ninjas
Little Ninjas Guitar Method Book
www.GuitarNinjas.com.au

Yellow Belt Rhythm

The **Beat** refers to the steady pulse of the music.

The **Rhythm** refers to the timing value of each individual note.

We're going to learn **Quarter Notes** which go for one count each.

We're also going to learn **Eighth Notes** which go for half a count. We need to put two Eighth Notes together to add up to the same value as one Quarter Note. This makes them sound twice as fast!

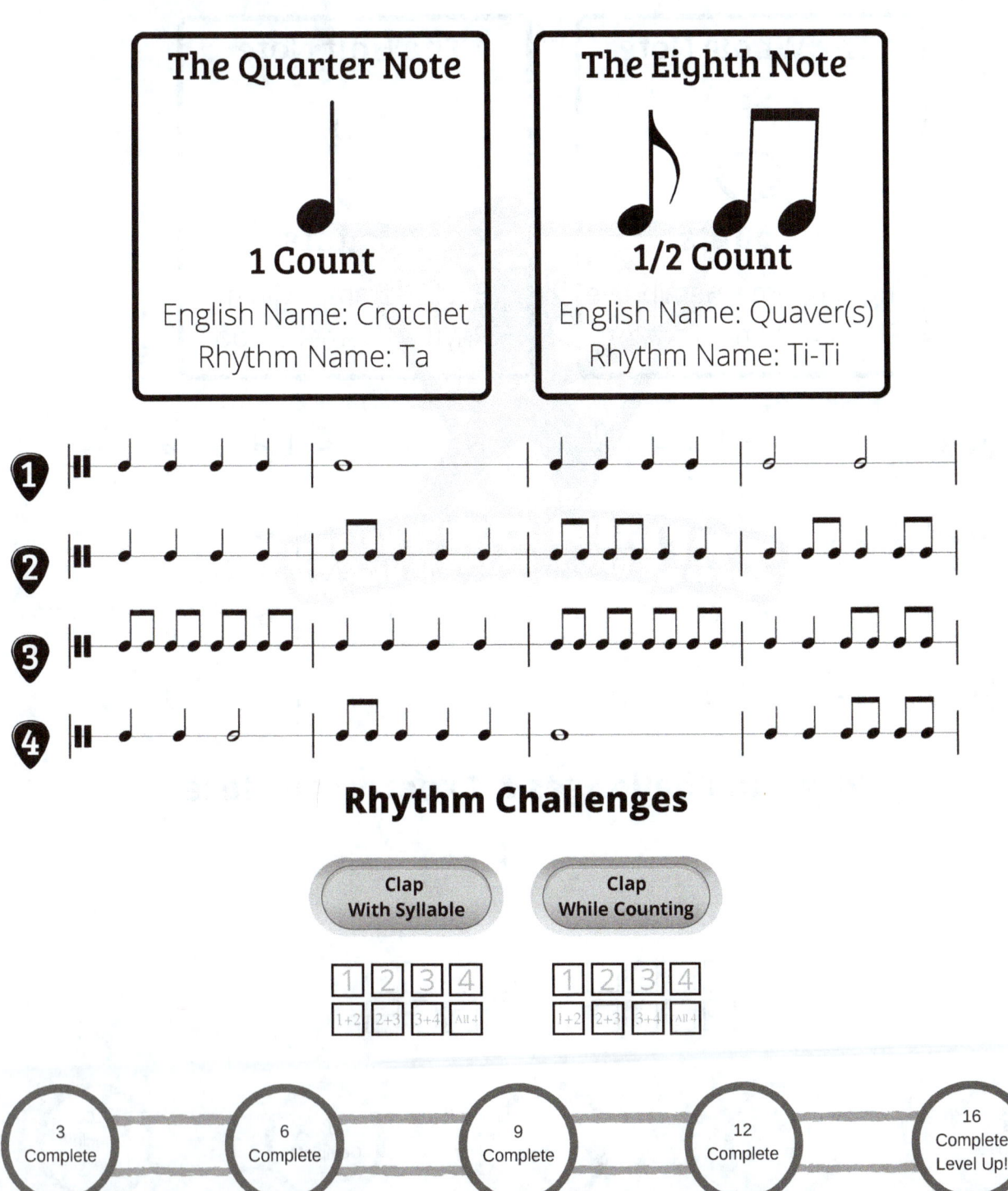

The Quarter Note
1 Count
English Name: Crotchet
Rhythm Name: Ta

The Eighth Note
1/2 Count
English Name: Quaver(s)
Rhythm Name: Ti-Ti

Rhythm Challenges

Clap
With Syllable

Clap
While Counting

1	2	3	4
1+2	2+3	3+4	All 4

1	2	3	4
1+2	2+3	3+4	All 4

3 Complete — 6 Complete — 9 Complete — 12 Complete — 16 Complete Level Up!

Orange Belt Rhythm

A **Rest** is used to indicate silence for a specific period of time. Essentially we are resting instead of playing a note

We've already learned four kinds of notes and will be learning the corresponding rests that share the same timing value.

A **Whole Note Rest** is shaped like a box and is found below the line, I like to imagine it is *'holding on'* to the line above.

A **Half Note Rest** is the exact same shape but is above the line, I like to think it is *halfway up* to the next line.

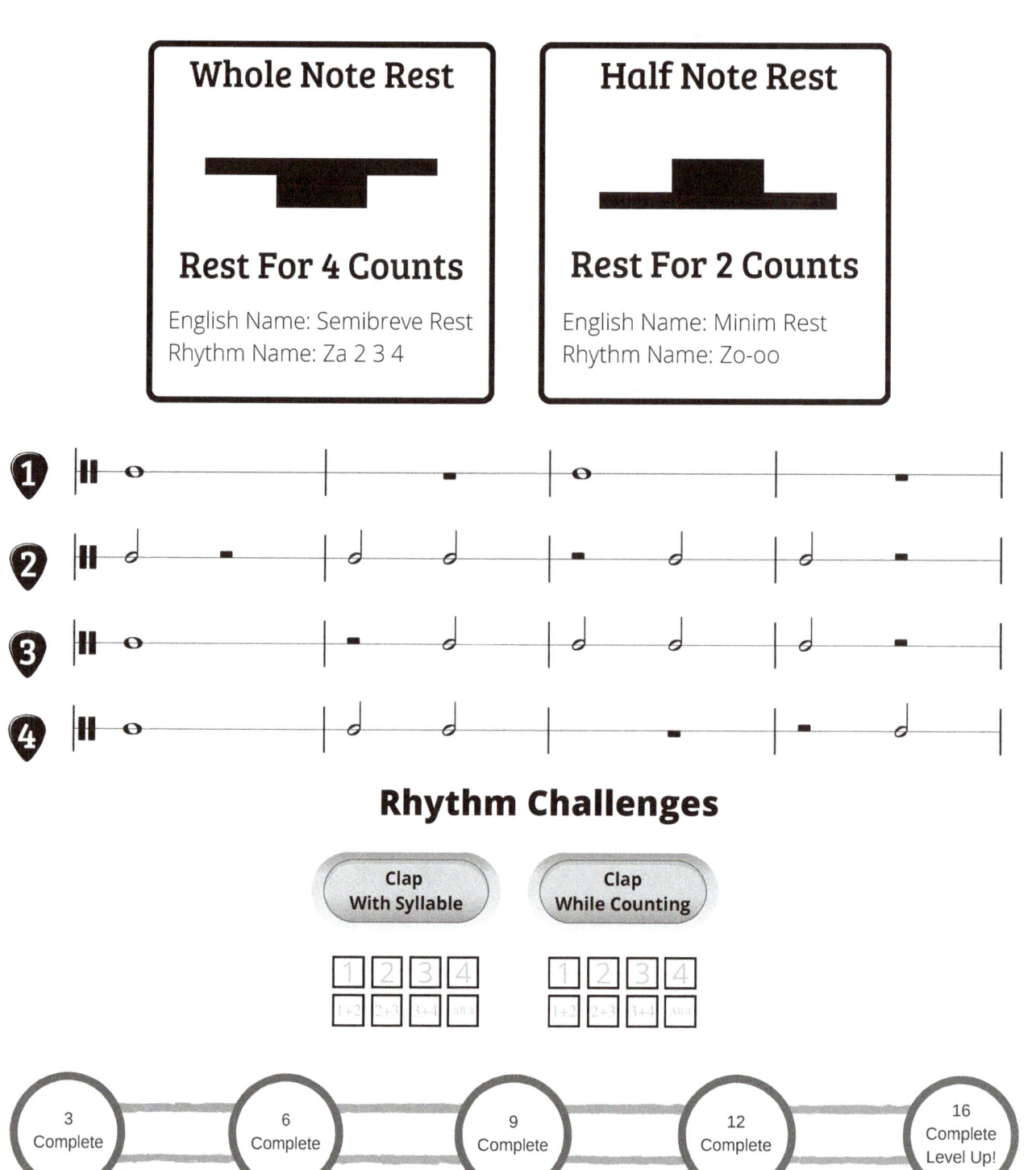

Whole Note Rest

Rest For 4 Counts

English Name: Semibreve Rest
Rhythm Name: Za 2 3 4

Half Note Rest

Rest For 2 Counts

English Name: Minim Rest
Rhythm Name: Zo-oo

Rhythm Challenges

Clap
With Syllable

Clap
While Counting

1	2	3	4
1+2	2+3	3+4	3+4

1	2	3	4
1+2	2+3	3+4	3+4

3
Complete

6
Complete

9
Complete

12
Complete

16
Complete
Level Up!

Green Belt Rhythm

A **Quarter Note Rest** indicates that we are resting for a period of one count. They look like a thunderbolt with a squiggly curl on the end. (I like to think of Harry Potter's thunderbolt shaped scar)

When clapping rhythms it can be helpful to open our hands up and have our palms face the roof whenever we have a rest so that our hands match the silence indicated by the rest.

When saying our rhythm syllable for Quarter Note Rests we use the word '**Za**' instead of 'Ta'

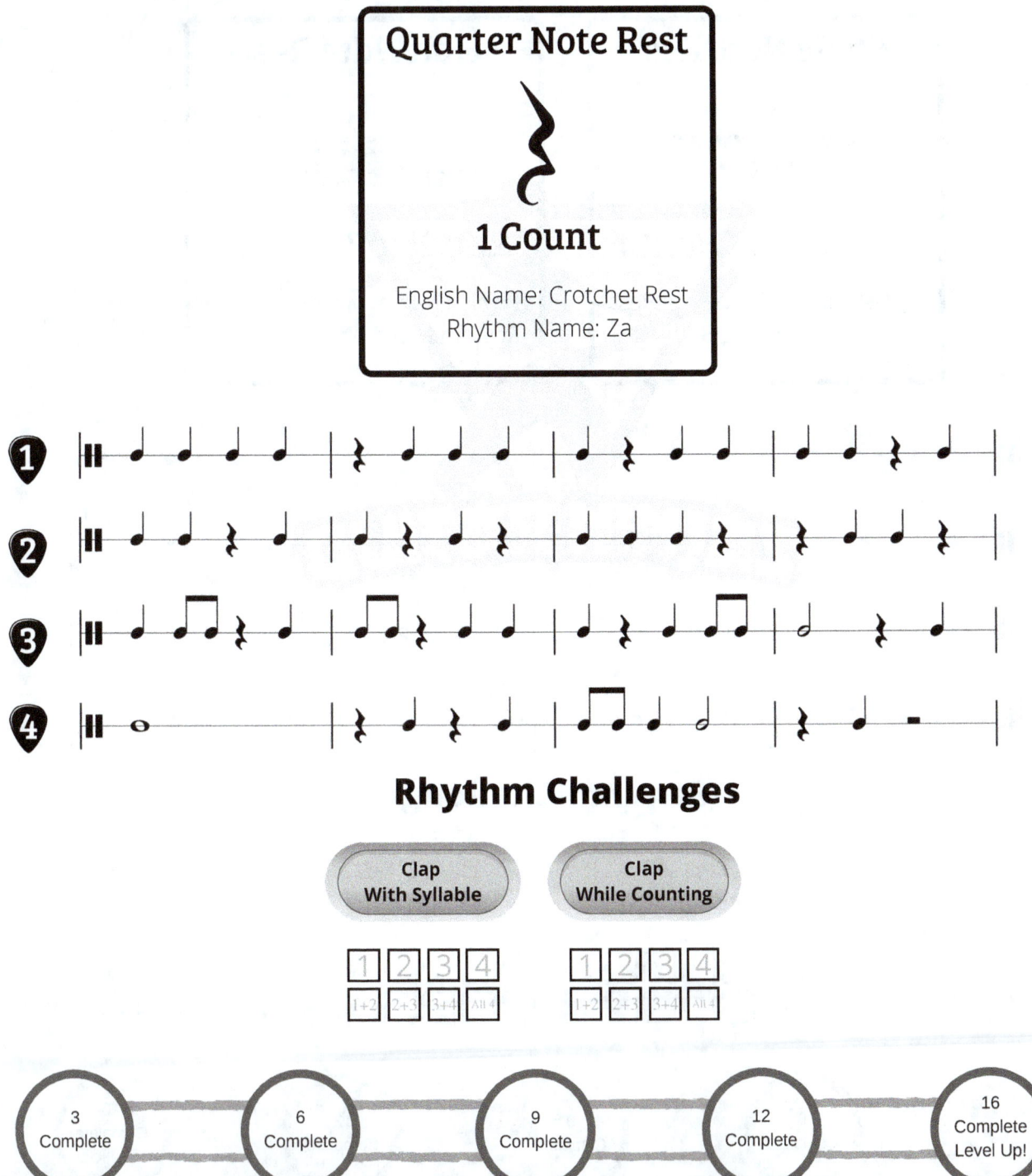

Rhythm Challenges

© Guitar Ninjas
Little Ninjas Guitar Method Book
www.GuitarNinjas.com.au

Blue Belt Rhythm

An **Eighth Note Rest** indicates that we are resting for a period of half a count.

We use the word **'Zi'** in place of 'Ti' when we say the rhythm syllable for Eighth Note Rests.

Eighth Note Rests are usually placed on the strong beats and allow us to highlight the offbeat. You'll need to get good at counting your offbeats when using Eighth Note Rests.

If we want to rest for two Eighth Notes, we will just use a Quarter Note rest because it goes for the full count.

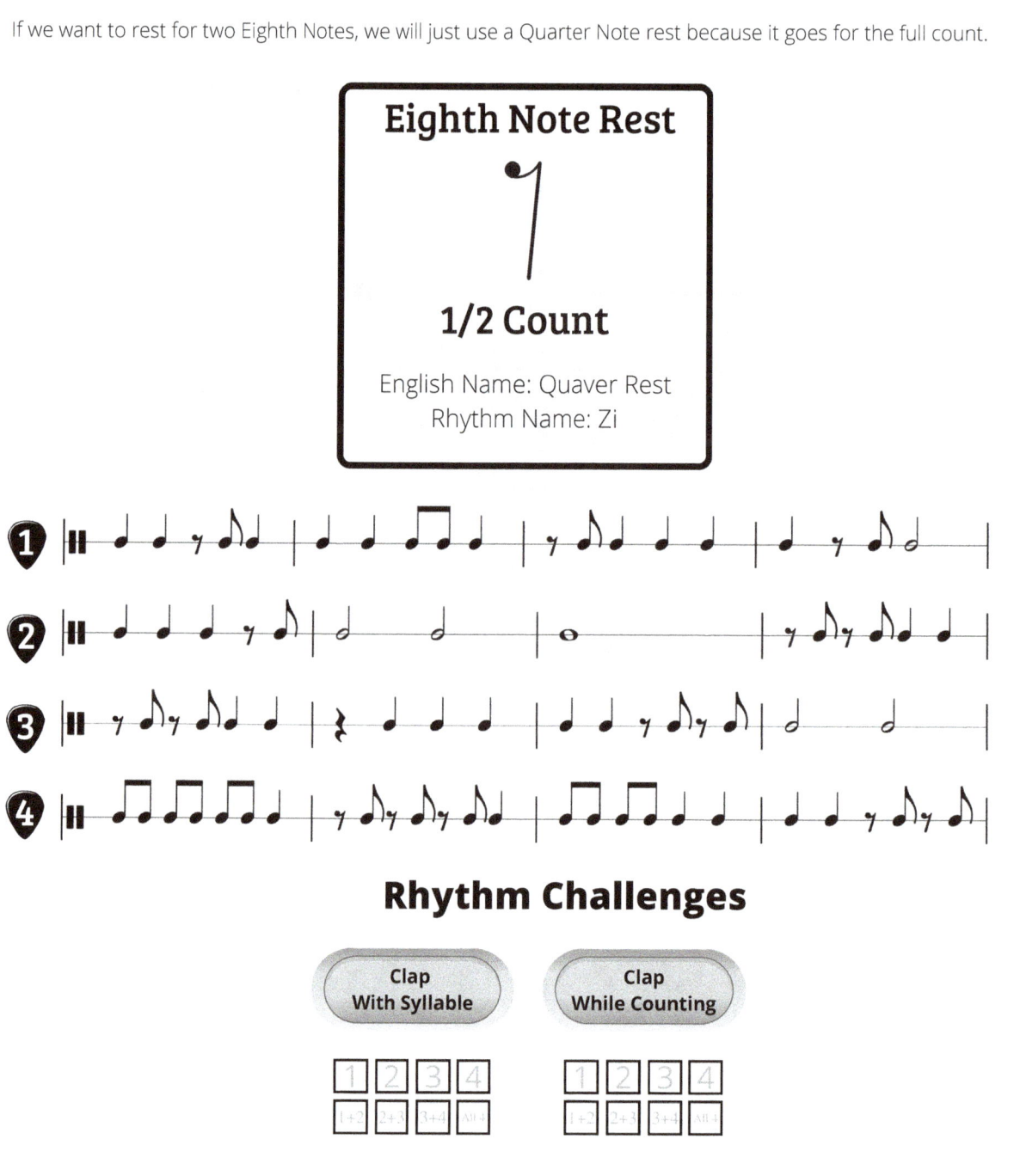

Rhythm Challenges

Purple Belt Rhythm

Notes that have a dot on them are called **Dotted Rhythms**. Adding a dot to a note extends the duration of a note by **half of the value**.

So if a Half Note goes for 2 counts, half of 2 is 1, and 2+1=3 therefore a **Dotted Half Note** goes for 3 counts.

If a Quarter Note goes for 1 count, half of 1 is .5, and 1+.5 = 1.5 therefore a **Dotted Quarter Note** goes for 1.5 counts.

The examples here will be given in **3/4 Time** meaning there will be **3 beats per bar**.

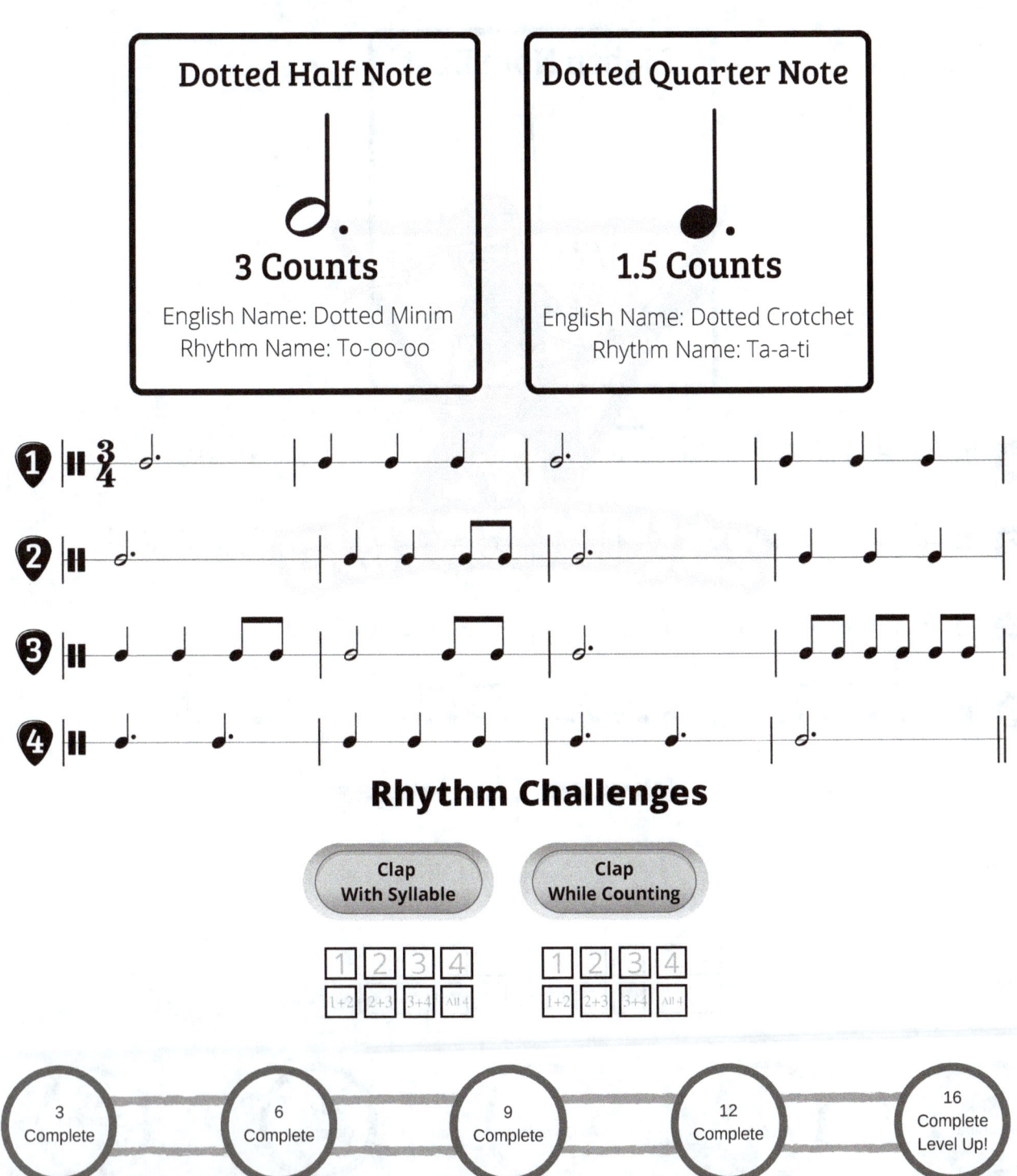

Dotted Half Note

3 Counts

English Name: Dotted Minim
Rhythm Name: To-oo-oo

Dotted Quarter Note

1.5 Counts

English Name: Dotted Crotchet
Rhythm Name: Ta-a-ti

Rhythm Challenges

Clap
With Syllable

Clap
While Counting

Red Belt Rhythm

A **Triplet** is a special kind of rhythm where we play three notes in the space of two. We usually put a small number 3 above the note symbol to indicate we are playing a triplet.

We can have **Half Note Triplets** where we play three Minims in the space of two. (four counts)

We can have **Quarter Note Triplets** where we play three Crotchets in the space of two. (two counts)

We can also have **Eighth Note Triplets** where we play three Quavers in the space of two. (one count)

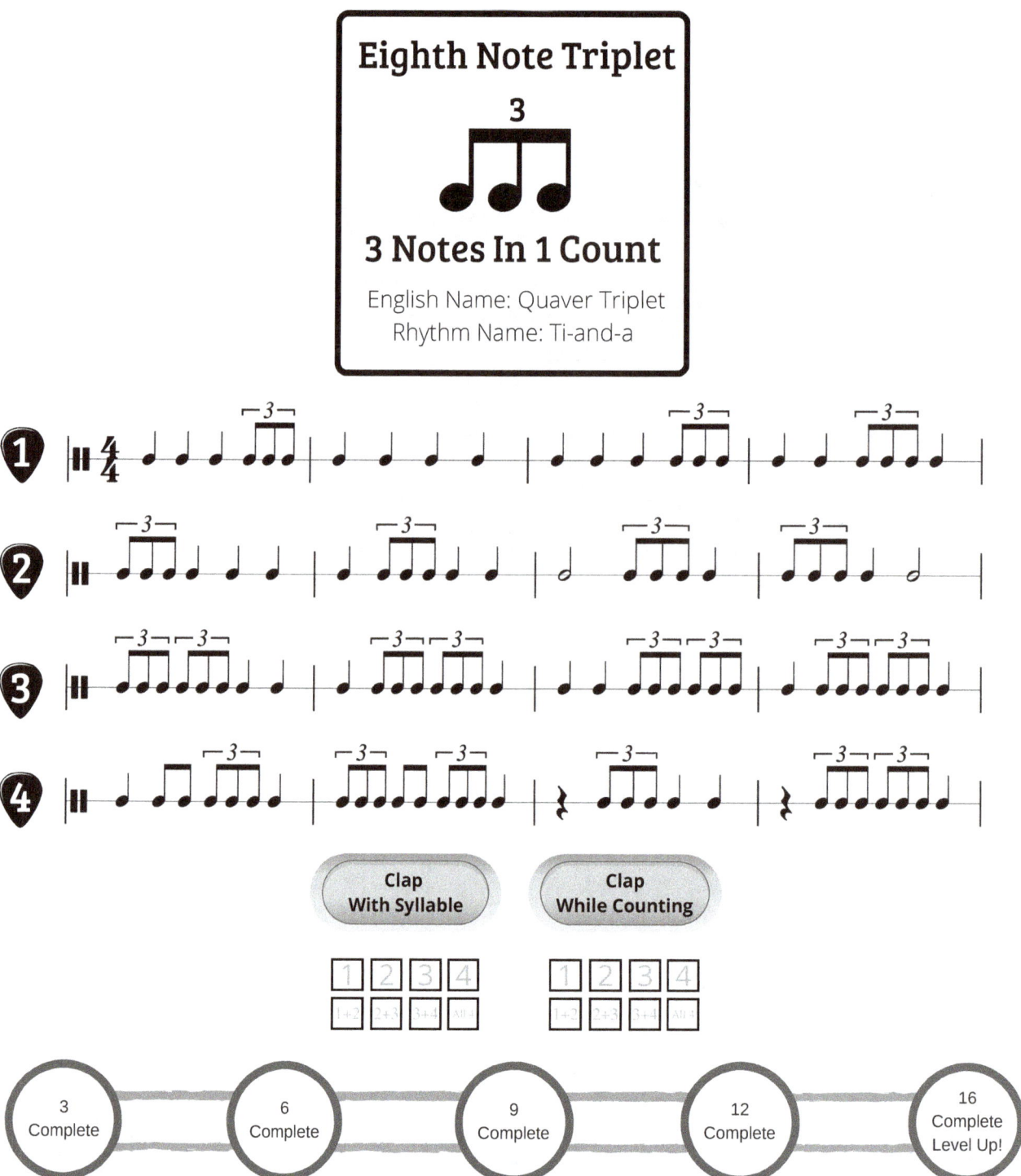

© Guitar Ninjas
Little Ninjas Guitar Method Book
www.GuitarNinjas.com.au

Grey Belt Rhythm

Notes that are linked together by a beam are called **Tied Notes**.

When we tie two notes together we are playing the first note for the duration of both notes added together.

We **Do Not** play the second note. We are simply adding its timing value to the original note to make it ring out for longer.

We can use tied notes within an individual bar of music, and to extend the duration of a note beyond the space of a single bar of music.

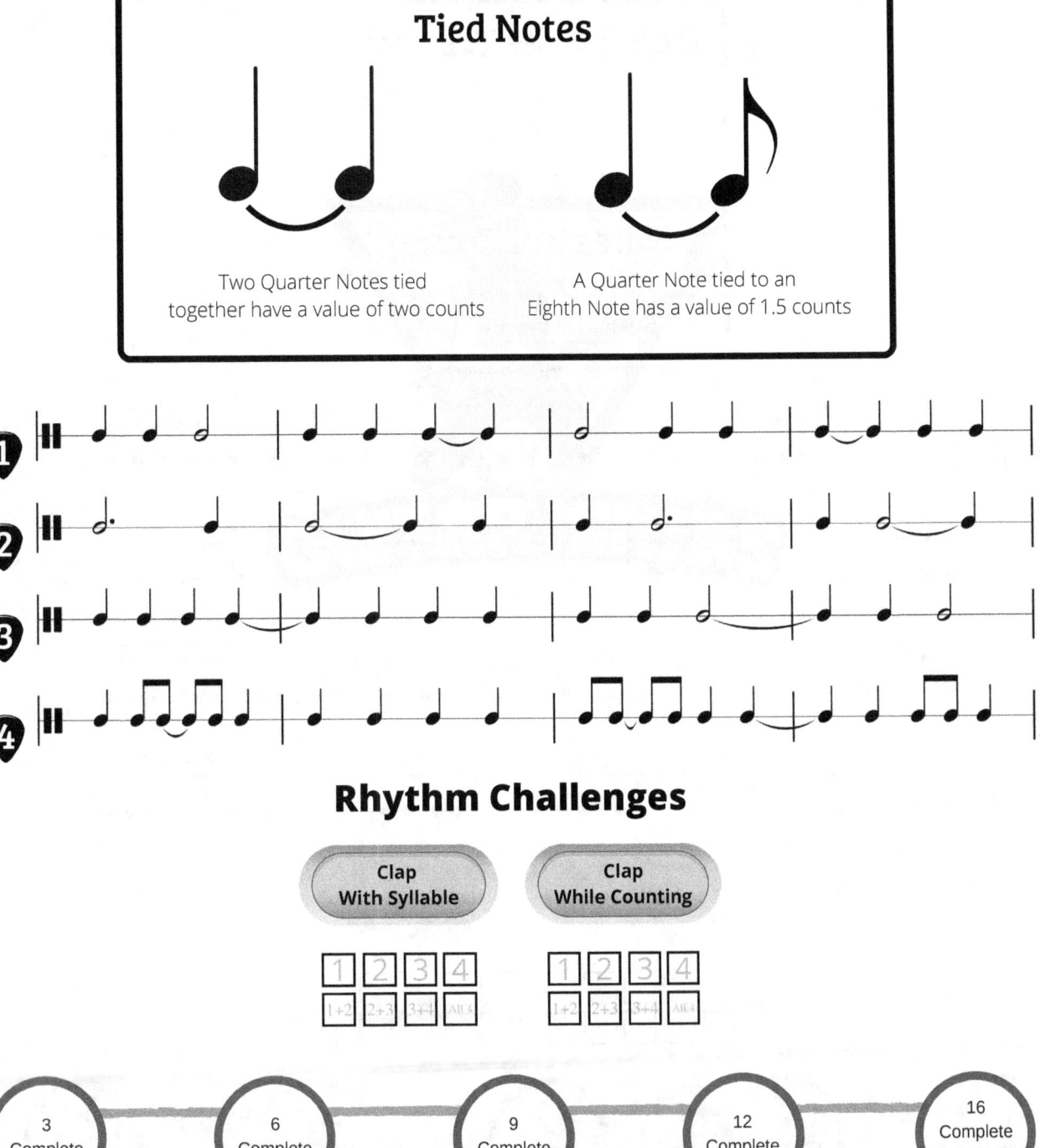

Tied Notes

Two Quarter Notes tied together have a value of two counts

A Quarter Note tied to an Eighth Note has a value of 1.5 counts

Rhythm Challenges

Clap With Syllable	Clap While Counting

3 Complete

6 Complete

9 Complete

12 Complete

16 Complete Level Up!

Black Belt Rhythm

If we take a whole note and break it in half we get two half notes. If we take a half note and break it in half we get two quarter notes. If we take a quarter note and break it in half we get an eighth note.

If we take an eighth note and break it in half we get a **Sixteenth Note**. We need two of them to match a single eighth note, and four of them to match a single quarter note.

This means that when we play Sixteenth Notes we play four notes in the space of a single beat. These will be a lot faster than what you're used to clapping so as you count 1-e-&-a or say ti-ka-ti-ka you may have to clap one your thighs.

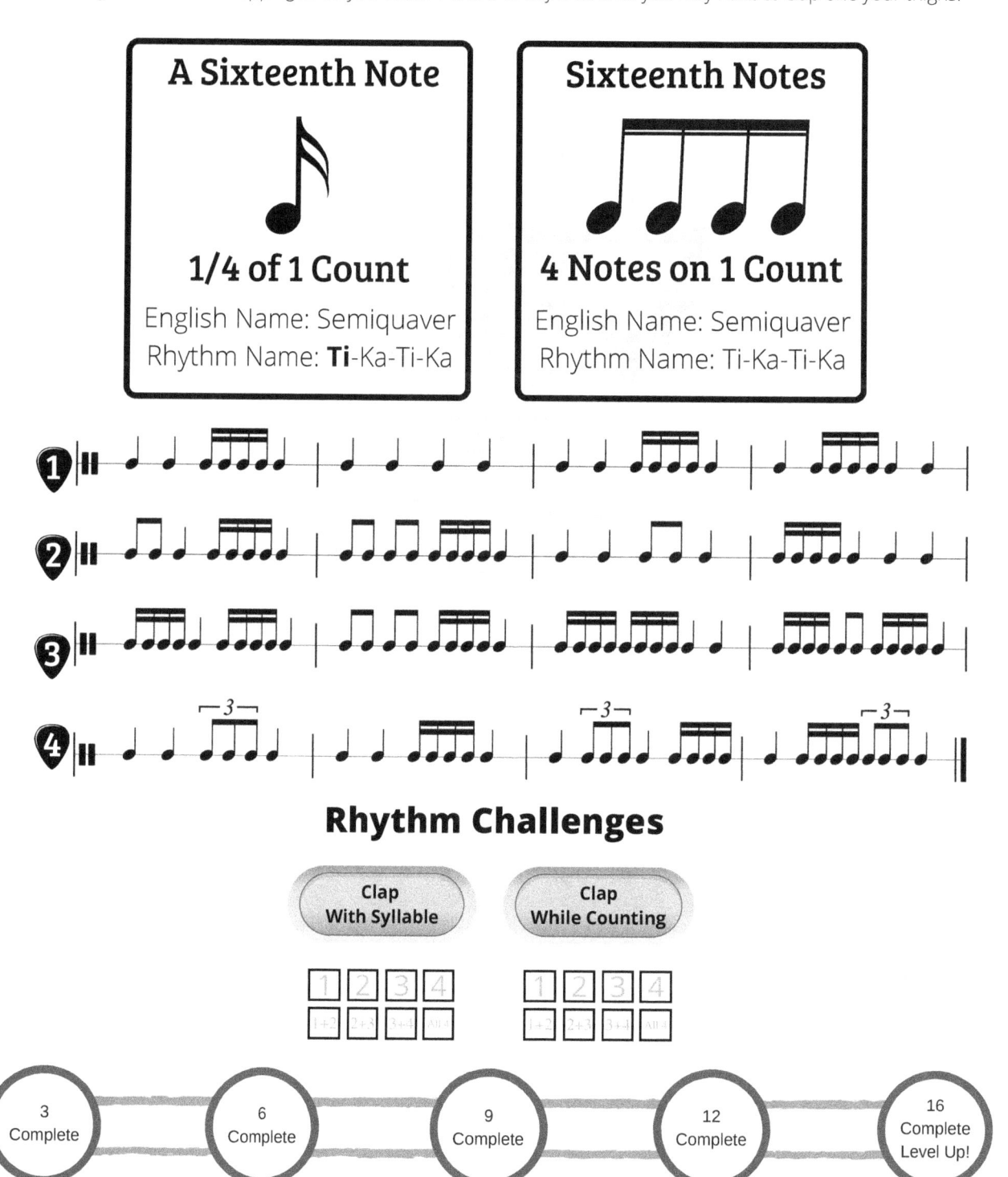

Rhythm Challenges

Section 7

Practice Log

The best way to get good at anything is to measure it.

In this section you will find a progress log for each level of your Guitar Ninjas journey.

You will also find a number of Practice Logs which you can fill in as you practice in order to keep a solid record of the time and effort you are putting in.

Practice Logs

On the next page there is a special practice log that you can use to record what you work in each of your practice sessions.

To record your practice simply put a tick next to the practice items you go through on that particular day.

For example if you practice riffs on the first day of the month, then put a tick or cross in the box next to riffs for that day.

If you do scales, riffs and chords on day 5, put a tick next to those items for that day, it's super simple to do.

In the event you want to track your actual practice time, just write the number of minutes you practised into the box instead of a tick. This will give you a great indication of where you spend your time and what areas might need a little more attention.

There are also some special practice challenges designed to help you practice efficiently and effectively. They don't count towards any level-ups, but they may lead to you getting real life prizes for working hard and practising lots.

Lastly, you can download and print off additional practice logs from www.GuitarNinjas.com.au once you complete the one in this book.

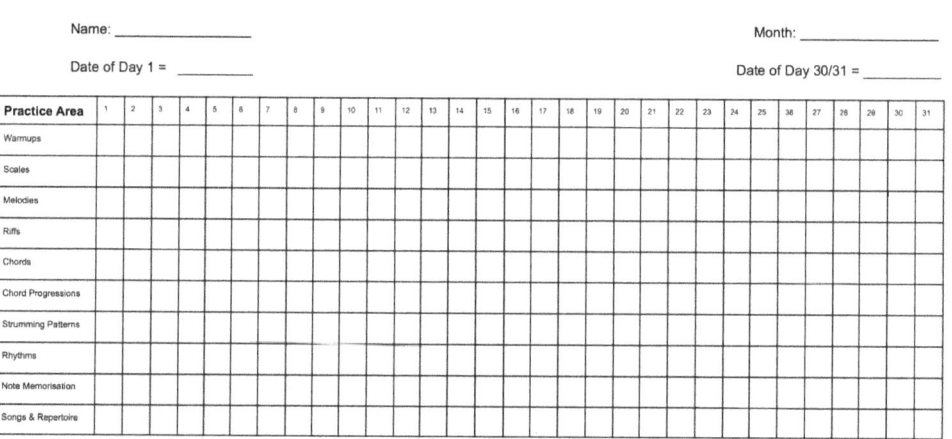

Little Ninjas Monthly Practice Log

Name: _____

Month: _____

Date of Day 1 = _____   Date of Day 30/31 = _____

Practice Area	1	2	3	4	5	6	7	8	9	10	11	12	13	14	15	16	17	18	19	20	21	22	23	24	25	26	27	28	29	30	31
Warmups																															
Scales																															
Melodies																															
Riffs																															
Chords																															
Chord Progressions																															
Strumming Patterns																															
Rhythms																															
Note Memorisation																															
Songs & Repertoire																															

3 Days In A Row — 1 complete

10 Days In A Row — 2 complete

15 Days In A Row — 3 complete

Practice On 20 Or More Days — 4 complete

Every Day Of The Month — 5 Complete Special Prize!

© Guitar Ninjas
Little Ninjas Guitar Method Book
www.GuitarNinjas.com.au

About The Author

Michael Gumley is a professional guitar teacher, author and musical educator from Melbourne, Australia. He founded Melbourne Guitar Academy in 2015 and has since authored 12 books on the topics of guitar playing and guitar teaching of which he's regarded as an expert on the topic. His proudest achievement is that his Guitar Ninjas curriculum is being used to train guitar players in music studios and guitar schools all around the world.

Michael began playing guitar at the age of 15 and was hooked from the very first (dead) note that he played. Often describing it like getting hit by a bolt of lightning - He knew instantly that he wanted to play the guitar for the rest of his life and (like many many teenagers who get the rock bug) would go on to practice up to 6 hours in pursuit of becoming the world's greatest guitarist.

Michael played in both cover and original bands while studying a Bachelor of Music and took lessons from some of Melbourne's best teachers. He also began attending guitar-playing events and teaching summits in the USA as his passion for guitar led him to pursue a full-time music & teaching career.

At the age of 25, he took the plunge and decided to commit to music full-time. After quitting his "*day job*" as a checkout chick at the local supermarket, he founded Melbourne Guitar Academy and has never looked back.

He is currently on the artist roster for Ormsby Guitars, Line 6 FX & Ernie Ball Strings, and has had past endorsement deals with ESP Guitars, Blackstar Amplification & Dean Markley Strings.

Michael looks to share his love of guitar & passion for music with each and every one of his students, and can't wait to help you with your guitar playing.

You can email Michael at info@GuitarNinjas.com.au or by following him on social media with the tag @MichaelGumley